Financial Fitness
For Young Adults

In God We Trust

Financial Fitness

7 simple steps to change your life for the better financially

For Young Adults

Yoli Marie

Financial Fitness Media, LLC

Copyright © 2009 by Yolanda Jackson

All rights reserved.

Cover design and book layout by Yvonne Matsumoto of Hill Rawls Marketing Consultants, LLC.

No portion of this book may be reproduced, stored in a retrieval system, or transmitted in any form or by any means— electronically, mechanical, photocopy, recording, scanning, or otherwise without permission of the publisher.

Published in Atlanta, Georgia by Financial Fitness Media, LLC.

Printed in the United States of America

ISBN: 978-0-615-30100-6

For book orders, author appearance inquiries and interviews contact the publisher at:

Financial Fitness Media, LLC

201 17th Street, Suite 300

Atlanta, GA 30363

Or via email: info@financialfitnessmedia.com

Acknowledgements

My book is dedicated in loving memory of my grandmother, Eva E. James. I would like to give honor to God for guiding my pathway to touch and change lives for the better financially. To my Mother, Barbara Plummer, I am grateful for your unconditional love, understanding and support. To my 14 year old brother, James Plummer, Jr., you inspire me to make the world a better place for you. I would like to extend gracious gratitude toward my friends and colleagues who encouraged me over every waking hour while I was writing and producing the book…Valerie Rawls, Yvonne Matsumoto, Howard Metcalf, Novel Scholars, Marshall Tyler, Sherry Andrew, Misscy Cage, Deardria Nesbitt, Evelyn Lynch, Scott Coleman, Joy Boyde, Denise Gines, Sherry Davis, Derek Motto (special thanks Derek for your book review and FINRA filing), Mc Daniel Austin, Don McGinnis, Laureen St. Clair, Esther Latham, and Duane Wilson.

Table of Contents

7 Simple Steps to Change Your Life For The Better Financially

About the Author
Page III

Introduction
Page V

CHAPTER 1:
Which Comes First? Money or Lifestyle?
Page 1

CHAPTER 2:
Plans for Spending
Page 29

CHAPTER 3:
Financial Wealth Check
Page 50

CHAPTER 4:
Debt or Pride?
Page 75

CHAPTER 5:
The Pulse of Your Credit Score
Page 93

CHAPTER 6:
Weigh In: Protect What You Value
Page 105

CHAPTER 7:
What does your legacy say about you?
Page 191

About the Author

Yoli Marie

Yoli Marie, author of "Financial Fitness For Young Adults, 7 Simple Steps To Change Your Life For The Better Financially" is a true trailblazer and financial genius who has the drive and determination to almost single-handedly save the next generation from financial despair. It is Yoli's belief that this generation of young adults between the ages of 18-24 can be the very first generation that has a record number of financially independent people before the age of 55. In uncertain economic times, a valuable personal finance book targeting young adults is worth more than 700 billion dollars! Yoli, with a heart-of-gold is committed to helping others and sharing her wealth of knowledge.

Meager beginnings growing up in the Dayton Street Housing Projects of Newark, NJ sculpted the desire for a better life, a financially independent life for Yoli. Immediately after high school she joined the Army and was stationed in Schofield Barracks, Hawaii, she was soon released on honorable discharge after two years of service. As a twenty year old Army Veteran, Yoli chose to follow her creative spirit; she lived her dream as an independent filmmaker for over nine years. There was no shortage of creativity but raising the capitol to get her short films off the ground was another challenge.

By chance or by destiny, in search of funding for one of her films, Yoli was introduced to an Investment Banker. After getting to know her, he suggested that she consider working in the world of money to learn how to speak and work with investors. Yoli took his advice and soon-thereafter became a Wall Streeter. This career opened a whole new world for Yoli including an opportunity to demystify personal money management, stocks, bonds, mutual funds; she couldn't wait to share this information with the world.

Yoli Marie was presented with the **President's Recognition for Quality of Advice Award** (2000) by the President of American Express Financial Advisors, David Huber, and has held several notable titles such as Investment Banker, Millennium Securities, Wall Street-New York City, Personal Financial Advisor and National Spokesperson for American Express Financial Advisors, VP of Wealth Management of the Atlanta Region for Colonial Bank, Columnist for **A-list Magazine, African-American Caribbean Newspaper** (NY), and has also been featured as one of **Ebony Magazine's** financial experts in the "**Money Talks**" column. Additionally, Yoli has been featured on the cable television station, **Oxygen**.

Yoli Marie is CEO of Financial Fitness Media, LLC (FFM) based in Atlanta, GA. Financial Fitness Media is a financial education company. Through creative multimedia, online and offline events FFM integrates financial education and pop culture with an emphasis on personal finance management, wealth creation and social responsibility.

For book orders or to hire Yoli Marie to speak, contact: Valerie Rawls, Hill Rawls Marketing Consultants, LLC, vrawls@hillrawls.com.

OUR INITIAL CONSULTATION

What led you here?

What led you here? Are you in search of the meaning of financial fitness? Looking for practical guidance to get your financial life in order? Are you questing to create a financially healthy "NEW YOU?"

I can get you there. From this point forward, I am your Personal Financial Fitness Coach. This book, "Financial Fitness For Young Adults, 7 Simple Steps To Change Your Life For The Better Financially," will guide you to create a valued lifestyle, get your finances straight and change your life for the better!

This book is interactive. Each chapter is like being in a one-on-one financial fitness coaching session with me. The chapters begin with coaching designed to educate you on financial matters that you need to know. Following the coaching session, you will be introduced to the interactive financial fitness workouts, your "homework" exercises. The financial workouts guide you on how to arrange your lifestyle and financial affairs. At the end of the workout, we will cool down for about 60 seconds so that you can wrap up your thoughts and completed workout. Then onto the next financial fitness coaching session!

Having a personal financial fitness coach is much like having a personal health and fitness coach. For example health and fitness trainers coach clients to change their lifestyle for the better health wise. They offer a health and fitness plan to exercise properly and achieve physical fitness goals, build strength and sustain increased endurance. Health and fitness trainers also promote better eating habits and healthier diets that enable clients to live at their best. In turn, their clients may experience results like enjoying a healthier lifestyle, participating comfortably in recreational and sporting activities, and let's not forget looking and feeling good!

Ideally there is no predefined moment when a person becomes physically fit. Becoming physically fit just happens overtime and it is ongoing. Because in order to become and remain physically fit, you have to continually work at it. All in all, having reasonable and attainable goals for your health and fitness spawns motivation and a road map to making changes in your health for the better. And so it is with financial fitness.

Financial fitness is also an ongoing journey on the road to better financial health. A financial fitness coach trains clients to change their lifestyle for the better financially. They coach clients to commit to one self and design a plan for living life at their best incorporating their most heart felt goals, dreams and aspirations.

Financial fitness promotes valuing your life, caring for your financial well being, exercising healthy spending habits and arranging your financial affairs the right way. Getting financially fit can help you sustain your lifestyle financially and increase your endurance to build wealth. In turn, as a result you will experience a fulfilled lifestyle while participating comfortably and secure in life financially.

There is no predefined level of wealth that signifies financial fitness. Financial fitness just happens overtime as you change your life for the better by living life at your best without sacrificing your financial wellbeing. And in order to remain financially fit, you have to continually work at it. What makes a financial fitness lifestyle worthwhile is pursuing passionate goals and modestly building wealth which will provide for long term financial security also known as financial freedom.

Imagine waking up each day having no worries about debt or your credit score's buying power, having plenty of money in the bank for living expenses, opportunities that may arise or unexpected financial emergencies. Imagine living life with no financial barriers, being able to make a difference in your community and most of all fulfill the goals and dreams that live within your heart. That is financial freedom. The 7 simple steps in this book can change your life for the better financially and put you on the road to financial freedom.

You need to have the desire to change your life for the better financially in order to benefit from this book. Just like most people know when they need to get physically fit, most people know when it is time to get financially fit. Where do you stand?

This book is an easy read. I purposely wrote the book that way. But I must give credit to the process for achieving financial freedom and mastering personal money management because it really is the easiest best kept secret, but not really a secret anymore.

Do you desire to learn everything you always wanted to know about getting fit financially and experiencing life with financial security? Perhaps, you did not learn the 7 simple steps to change your life for the better financially in school or at home, but you now hold the keys to a financial fitness lifestyle and achieving financial freedom.

Calling Attention to Young Adults

I've specifically written this book with the intention to communicate with young adults. It is my belief this generation of young adults between the ages of 18-35 can be the very first generation that has a record number of financially independent people before the age of 55. This can be the first generation to redefine retirement age and I am not speaking of redefining Social Security or Medicare. I mean retiring because you can by age 55 You are earning a historical level of income upwards of $50,000, $70,000 and $100,000 or more in annual income within the first few years out of college and more annual income beyond. While other generations fought and won freedom from oppression, civil and social liberties, you are the generation that will gain wealth!

Young people, you may be the first wealth generation, but let's be honest, you do not know what to do with the economic opportunity that you've earned. It is not your fault either. For the most part, you are not getting the attention that you deserve or guidance on how to arrange your lifestyle financially and achieve financial freedom before you spend it all.

What is getting a hold of your generation's attention as a result? The consumer goods retail market. Wealth building organizations like mutual fund companies, insurance companies, and other financial corporations just don't have the same advertising spending.

Financial literacy is a global challenge. In my opinion, practical money management and wealth building lessons should be taught in grades K-12 on their respective grade levels then followed up at the university level. There are some school districts beginning to incorporate teaching children and teens about basic money management skills. That is a wonderful step toward financial literacy. When all children and teens are taught financial literacy programs and the importance in achieving financial freedom, we will have the greatest number of financially independent people in the world changing the economic landscape for generations to come.

Who will stand up and be responsible for showing young adults what to do with the inherited economic opportunity and put them on the right track by steering them away from instant gratification, materialism and debt? Who will stand up and show the young people how to create wealth and achieve financial freedom by the time they're age 55 so that they can enjoy a better retirement lifestyle than the previous generation did?

Starting now, with this book I will stand up for you and support you in achieving financial freedom. My goal is to help an infinite number of young adults change their lives for the better financially beginning with this book and more to come. I will not rest until I get a chance to meet you in your city and share information and financial resources with you hands on.

About Me, Yoli

I want you to know that I was once like you. Not really sure about how to get my financial life in order. I got caught up in debt issues and have been broke moving through life trying to get a hold of my money. My family was by no means well to do. After all, we lived in the Dayton Street Housing Projects of Newark, NJ when I was a little girl.

I was the third generation to live in the housing projects with my family. Some relatives moved out before my mother moved us out. Later, my grandmother and other relatives made it out of the projects to better neighborhoods. Nonetheless, while living on Dayton Street, I do recall my grandmother, Eva James, trying to teach me something about money when I was a little girl. My grandmother was teaching me how to be responsible by putting some money in the bank first, then pay bills before spending money on other things. She taught me by example.

When I was 7 years old, each Friday after school I would meet my grandmother at her job which was walking distance from our housing projects. She worked at the local factory that produced hair accessories for women like bobby pins, hair nets, barrettes and pony-tail holders. On our way home from my grandmother's job, we would stop at the bank so that she could cash her check and put money into her savings account. She would show me her savings account passbook and teach me the transaction process with the bank teller. Then on our way home we would go to McDonald's for dinner. That was my Friday treat. When we got home, she would have me sit on the bed next to her, open the dresser drawer and pull out several white envelopes. Then she'd reach into her purse and pull out the bank's envelope. She would look at me and say something like this, "See here, each time you get paid from your job you first put some money in the bank then put a little money on your bills. So today, I am putting some money in the rent envelope and the light bill envelope." She told me when it was time to pay the bill; she would always have enough saved in the envelope for it.

Did your family members teach you similarly? Like my family, did they also instill in you good grades and a college education will get you a decent paying job or rewarding career? And were you also taught to put some money away for a rainy day? I hope so, but even then, were you like me and thought that something was missing?

I will tell you what was missing for me. To live in a house in a nice neighborhood, being able to escape the 15 mile radius of my community and travel to fancy places and have other experiences. I also always wondered what the stock market is. To me the stock market was mentioned on news reports that would interrupt my favorite radio show but I was ignorant to the significance of the report at the time.

I knew there were some members of my family who "moved on up" like the Jefferson's. Why didn't my immediate family? I was told that good grades and a college education will get you a decent paying job or rewarding career. What I wasn't told was how do I buy a house and escape the projects? How do I make my money grow and never be poor again? How do I retire with wealth and afford better healthcare options in my golden years? How do I live the American dream!

I joined the US Army directly following high school and was stationed in Hawaii. I joined to earn money for a college education, but I also wanted to go to Hawaii for other reasons. As a little girl, Hawaii was my dream escape from my world. Some children had imaginary friends. I had an imaginary life in Hawaii. Hawaii symbolized paradise to me. I served a two year enlistment in the US Army and became an Army Veteran at the age of 20. Then I went to college.

Two years after returning home from the military my grandmother passed away. She had heart disease; she died at age 62 within hours after having surgery at a public hospital in Newark, NJ. My grandmother received healthcare benefits through Medicaid and I knew then that meant she may not have had access to the best possible health care options. I began to obsess and think: What if my grandmother was wealthy? Would she be alive today because she could have afforded the best health care in America? What might happen to me if I do not have a certain level of wealth and health care options in my retirement years, I will have to accept a lower standard of health care options too. It was then that I began to realize the importance of having financial security. I wanted to have a good quality lifestyle and the freedom with no financial barriers. At age 22, I had no idea how to make that happen. I had no answers. I knew of no resources.

Since then, I did whatever it took to find the answers. It took me many, many years of hard learned lessons and searching. I did not initially pursue a career in financial services. My first passion was to become a filmmaker like Spike Lee. I was inspired by Spike

Lee to write and direct films. I followed my creative spirit and worked as an independent filmmaker until the age of 29. It was while I was planning to make a low budget movie and raise capital from investors, Wall Street found me.

I was comfortable with the creative demands of filmmaking, but raising money for my project was a different story. I had no earthly idea how to start. More than that, I was terrified to ask investors for money. I was taught as a child that you do not ask people details about their money or to borrow money. I had a money block, not a creative block.

Fortunately, I was led to an introduction with an investment banker. Since investment bankers work in the world of money, I thought I'd ask for his advice on how to raise capital. He suggested, "Why don't you become an investment banker and you can learn about money, Wall Street, and how to meet and speak to investors who can potentially invest in your project?

There was a lot of hard work in store for me as I trained to become an investment banker. I loved every minute of it because I finally found the answers to financial freedom! I was absorbing everything I needed to know about my new career, like a sponge. Yes, my new career.

Filmmaking remains in my heart but I found a new sweetheart career—Wall Street. What was seemingly a mystery and is a mystery for the average person today was no longer so for me. I demystified Wall Street, personal money management, stocks, bonds, mutual funds, all of it. I instantly became excited to share this information with people. I am so enthusiastic about teaching people the 7 simple steps to change your life for the better financially, how to build wealth modestly and become financially secure. I knew if I could learn it, you can too.

So let me ask you again, what led you here today? What is missing in your life? Do you really want to know how to create a quality lifestyle and build financial freedom so that you can enjoy life with no financial barriers? Would you be willing to do whatever it takes to achieve financial freedom? Are you ready and willing to commit to following the 7 simple steps in this book that will change your lifestyle for the better financially?

Young people, I promise you 3 things: I will not bore you, I will not use wacky jargon, I will coach you to financial fitness.

7 Simple Steps to Change Your Life For The Better Financially

A Prelude

The seven simple steps to change your life for the better financially lie within seven motivating one-on-one financial coaching sessions.

1. **Which Comes First? Money or Lifestyle?**
   I don't want to give the answer away!

2. **Plans For Spending**
   Cha-ching, Cha-ching, Cha-ching! This coaching session will expand your awareness of spending so that you can grab a hold of your finances and make your money work better for you.

3. **Financial Wealth Check**
   Did you know your self esteem relates to how well you build wealth? I will unveil the moving parts of the formula in this chapter.

4. **Debt or Pride?**
   Is debt stronger than pride? Find your own answers within this coaching session.

5. **The Pulse Of Your Credit Score**
   When was the last time you checked the pulse of your credit score? Is it dead or alive and well? I can teach you how to revive it and make it stronger. Read here.

6. **Weigh In: Protect What You Value**
   If I showed you how to protect your lifestyle from a financial storm, would you? Get coached on how to protect yourself from unpredictable financial setbacks.

7. **What does your legacy say about you?**
   Your legacy is not about how much money you have or leave behind when you die. It is about you and the impact you make on the lives of others whether negative or positive. How do you want to be remembered? Our final financial fitness coaching session is all about enjoying determining what your legacy will be!

Chapter 1

Which Comes First? Money or Lifestyle?

I polled the question which comes first, money or lifestyle? I asked hundreds of young adults and here are a couple of my favorite responses:

Brittany, age 27

"Lifestyle comes first. You have to have that in mind, and then have a plan to get it and sustain it. I've always known what I wanted for my life. And I know what I need to do to get it. You know what you are willing to put up with. If you are not satisfied or not where you want to be, make more money. You have the ability to change your lifestyle."

Mark, age 31

"Money comes first. Money should dictate your lifestyle. Money should dictate whether you stay within your means. Goal wise, I look at lifestyle. I use that to set my goals. For the immediate I look at money first because I don't want to go bankrupt living beyond my means. You don't want to put your lifestyle first because it will be a constant struggle."

What is your answer? Money or lifestyle first?

Overall the poll confirmed for me that there is a mixed message young adults are receiving about what is a lifestyle and how money relates to it. The perception of the majority of young people polled was, their lives are absent of a lifestyle unless or until they have money to plug into "buying" the lifestyle they desire. Their perception is a misconception.

Lifestyle isn't a gift waiting for you to arrive to get it. Young people you are not on hold waiting for the right time for lifestyle to show up in your life. You have the gift of life already and you are living your life in your own style right now at this moment. There are no qualifications for having a lifestyle. Your lifestyle is what you make it in the present moment and how you live it.

Lifestyle is simply a way of living. Each of us live our life in a unique way. Similarly, we are seeking to fulfill the same needs, food, clothing, shelter, goals, hobbies, interests, social interaction, and financial security.

Your uniqueness is demonstrated by your choices, your family values, and your community. What you wear, the foods you eat, your hobbies and experiences, your social circle, your worship and career also signals how you want to live your life. These are the ingredients of "your" unique lifestyle.

Money is just a resource to finance your lifestyle. Money does not decide what kind of lifestyle is best for you. You do. You dictate how you will live now and in the future. You make the plans for your life then use money as a resource to finance your plans. If more money than you have is needed to finance a more desirable lifestyle, it is up to you to employ time and energy to generate the monetary supply you need. Like love is not for sale, money can't buy lifestyle.

So the winner is? Lifestyle. Lifestyle comes first, then money. However, the relevant question is: How are you living? Are you living your best life and choosing to invest your time, energy, and money on what matters most to you?

> **CHANGE YOUR LIFE
> FOR THE BETTER FINANCIALLY**
>
> **Simple Step #1:
> Design a Plan for
> Living Life at Your Best**

Changing your life for the better financially does not begin with looking at how much debt you got yourself into or how much money you do or do not have at this moment. By the time you finish this book, you will understand everything there is to know about financial fitness.

For now, turn finances off in your mind. Lifestyle comes first. Before pursuing money and getting your financial affairs straight, you must first design a plan for living life at your best defined by your values, and a sense of purpose with passionate goals. First know what you want from your life. Value your lifestyle. Have the courage to make change and do better. Then invest your time, energy and money in your life's plans and goals, your lifestyle. Do this without sacrificing your financial well being. Living a financial fitness lifestyle can help you accomplish this.

Financial Fitness, A Lifestyle

Financial fitness is a way of living—a lifestyle. Financial fitness is not only about keeping your money straight. Financial fitness is creating and sustaining the lifestyle that you desire without sacrificing your financial health and ability to achieve financial freedom.

Financial fitness is the opposite of:

- My life is dull and meaningless.
- I don't know where my money is going.
- I can't seem to get ahead financially.
- I have "bling bling," sky miles, expensive toys, but no financial security.
- I live a borrowed lifestyle, on credit cards.
- I am not concerned about how my actions impact others.

Financial Fitness is:

- I am passionately pursuing what I want to experience in life.
- I put my time, energy, and money on what matters most to me.
- I am modestly building wealth year after year.
- I volunteer my time, talent or positively impact the lives of others.
- I value my lifestyle and financial freedom.
- I protect what I value.

Most people know when their financial health and wellness is not up to par or in jeopardy. The awareness stems from feeling insecure financially, spending a lot of time and energy worrying about paying bills, fear of running out of money, and their debt load. Unfortunately for some people, not enough time and energy is spent on changing for the better and getting financially fit. This does not mean that people lack the desire to be financially secure or are without knowledge of the basic principles of financial fitness. Everyone knows living within your means, saving, and resisting credit card usage are healthy financial habits even if disregarded.

So what is really getting in the way of people living a financial fitness lifestyle? Distractions. Distractions from what matters most to them, distractions from valuing what matters most, distractions from designing a plan for their life and distractions that sacrifice their financial well being. However, you can regain control of the direction of your lifestyle and financial matters by taking the bull by the horns and confronting distractions head on. You owe it to yourself because you absolutely deserve a fulfilling financially secure life.

The fact that you are reading this book tells me that changing your life for the better financially is important to you. Now is your time to seize the moment to improve your financial health so that you are able to comfortably live a fulfilling lifestyle. You need to pursue your goal to change your life for the better financially with the same fervor, zest, and determination as any other undertaking in your life. Actually, you have no option but to take an active role in effectively managing your lifestyle.

Your Lifestyle's Valued Purpose

Your values are the silver lining of your life and basis of your actions and decisions. Values are principles and standards that you highly regard. Even though you may not realize it, your values influence the way you approach and execute your life. Valuing a healthy body leads a person to exercise regularly and choose to eat healthy foods. In the same way, if you value family, chances are you make certain to be in close touch or spend quality time with family members. You may value integrity. Therefore you are truthful and honest in all of your dealings and are likely to admire others who demonstrate the same. We live by our values and become what we value.

If you value your lifestyle, you are living your life in a healthy way physically, spiritually, as well as financially. If you value your lifestyle you live with passion and a sense of purpose making conscious choices about how you invest your time, energy, and money.

What purpose drives you passionately? Purpose can be defined in many ways. I am referring to purpose in the concrete sense involving deliberate thoughts and actions. Purpose is deliberate thought through goal directedness. Purpose is something that passionately drives you with interest and intrigue giving you the feeling and need to continue to grow, experience life and achieve desired results. This is the birth place of your short term and long term goals.

Intuitively, most people know what life experiences, goals and dreams are in their heart. However, if you do not value pursuing what you want to experience in life and lack a burning desire to commit to your heart's desires, then your goals and dreams may be chalked up as "wishful thinking." Life will simply pass you by. You will end up wasting your energy and money on a style of life that is less gratifying and most importantly fritter away your life's time---lifetime.

Time, Energy, and Money (T.E.M.)

Not all of your goals will require money. Some may require more of your time than money. Others time, energy and money. T.E.M. are precious resources. How well you manage T.E.M. will depend on your values and how passionate you are about your goals. For example, if you invest T.E.M. on any purpose that is not aligned with what matters most to you, does not support your values, goals or is something you do not feel passionate about, you are wasting it. Essentially, you are distracted and holding yourself back from living the lifestyle that you really want. That same T.E.M. wasted will always add up exponentially in your favor when you invest it wisely in what matters most to you. Wisely investing in "YOU" can change your life for the better.

The Courage to Make Change And Do Better

To change your life for the better in any area of your life, you will need to make a change in the way you are living. There are many people who have decided to forego setting goals and making changes for the better in their life because they have become frustrated with the challenges or failures they've experienced. I understand how easily you can get discouraged and throw in the towel. However, it is within this moment of discouragement you can find your greatest lesson. You can learn from your mistakes and seek other ways to overcome your challenges and experience a different outcome. Thomas Edison said, "I was never a failure. I had 2000 chances to get it right." Thankfully Thomas Edison kept trying; we now have light bulbs!

There is another famous quote that says, "Insanity is doing the same thing over and over, and expecting a different result." You can easily drive yourself crazy doing the same thing over and over expecting a different result! If you continue to do things the same way, continue living the same way, you will get the same result you've always gotten. It only makes sense to try a different way to accomplish the result you are looking for. Right?

Ask any successful person about achieving desired results or goals. They will tell you that the discipline to be an early riser, work hard, stay focused to accomplish anything does not come easily. Success just does not happen that easy. After all we have distractions of all sorts to contend with and a routine life to live. In the midst of it all, sometimes our intentions may get overlooked. When this happens, it does not mean you are a bad person, lazy, or not intelligent. It means you are living in an environment with compelling distractions. I bet you can name 10 distractions that exist in your daily environment with no problem!

Distractions may be the company you keep, places you go, the things that you do and competition for your money in the consumer market arena. Even more powerfully, your number one distraction may be YOU because you have the power to change and do better. Believe that you can, pursue change and achieve your desired outcome. Can you commit to courageously make positive changes in your life so that you can enjoy financial security?

Redefine Your Lifestyle

No matter your life stage or how messy your financial house is today, you can get on the track to financial fitness and turn your life around. Starting today, you can begin to remove distractions in your environment and redefine what you want from your life.

Redefining and discovering how you would like to live your life can be liberating. You are the architect of your lifestyle. You are in charge of designing and expanding your unique lifestyle inspired by interests, goals and dreams that live within YOU. Only you know what that looks like and how you would feel experiencing it. So it is up to you to design a lifestyle that you will enjoy now and in your future without sacrificing your financial well being.

You will not change your life for the better financially overnight, but you can overtime. I know you can. Just remember financial fitness is a lifestyle, a way of living. You can't just try financial fitness. You have to commit to apply financial fitness to your daily living. As you learn the seven simple steps to financial fitness in this book and complete each financial workout, you will witness your financial fitness lifestyle shape up with increased clarity.

Are you ready? If you think you are ready. YOU are. It's not 'can this book' change your life for the better financially, but can YOU?

Redefine what you want from your life. Design a plan for your best life. This is a fun and refreshing step in creating a financial fitness lifestyle. Out with the old and in with the new you!

Your First Financial Fitness Workout:
Design A Plan For Living Life At Your Best

This is your first financial workout. I am excited to share this step with you for it is my favorite financial fitness topic. I enjoy coaching people to create lifestyles filled with fulfilling experiences and accomplishments. I love this topic because each and every time I am coaching someone I learn something fascinating. I learn what is in their hearts, their dreams, what brings joy, and what is missing in their life. Most of all, I am reminded of how unique we are individually.

During this workout, I will coach you through five simple steps that will challenge yourself to answer:

1. What do I value most in life?
2. What do I stand for?
3. What does my best life look like in all areas of my life?
4. What are my most heart felt interests or goals that I would like to experience or accomplish in the short term and long term?
5. What action will I need to take to live my life according to my values, what I stand for, and my true goals.

Ultimately, the self discovery processes will rebirth a purpose for living in all areas of your life. There are six key areas of your life that may uniquely house your purpose:

1. Career/Professional
2. Community
3. Family/Relationships
4. Financial
5. Personal Development
6. Spiritual

What does your best life look like in each area? How are you living life in these areas now? Are you living by default going with the flow according to someone else's expectations or are you challenging yourself to pursue interests and goals that live deep inside of you? Do you have goals or special interests on the shelf collecting dust? What is missing in your life? What is going well as planned? This is the moment to be honest with YOU. No penalty is involved here. The prize is for YOU to recognize where you are today and take courageous steps to live life at your best.

Step One: Identify Your 5 Core Values

Identifying your values is a meaningful step that will help you stay focused on what is important to you ensuring your actions and decisions are aligned with your values now and in the future. This exercise will help you identify your 5 core values and what you stand for. When you are done, evaluate whether past actions or decisions reflect your values.

1. From the list of values below write your top 20 values on the next page.
2. Next narrow your top 20 values to 10. Put a check-mark next to your top ten values.
3. Lastly, narrow your top ten values to 5. Circle your 5 core values.

VALUES:		
Achievement	Fairness	Loyalty
Arts	Faith	Merit
Adventure	Fame	Peace
Balance	Financial Freedom	Personal
Change	Financial Security	Philanthropy
Community	Freedom	Power
Courage	Happiness	Privacy
Creativity	Health-Wellness	Quality
Development	Helping-Others	Relationships
Discipline	Honesty	Respect
Diversity	Independence	Social Responsibility
Education	Inner Peace	Spirituality
Ethics	Integrity	Stability
Excellence	Leadership	Wealth
Family	Learning	Wisdom

Chapter 1: What Comes First? Money or Lifestyle?

Your top 20 values:

1.	
2.	
3.	
4.	
5.	
6.	
7.	
8.	
9.	
10.	
11.	
12.	
13.	
14.	
15.	
16.	
17.	
18.	
19.	
20.	

Step Two: Brainstorm

Brainstorm, brainstorm, brainstorm. Brainstorming is a process for developing creative ideas or solutions. It works best when you focus on an isolated issue, deliberately coming up with as many ideas or solutions as possible without censoring any.

On six separate sheets of paper, write one of the six key areas of your life at the top of the page. Begin in any order that you wish. And then brainstorm. Do this for each key area of your life.

Activate your imagination and brainstorm about what you would like to experience or accomplish in the six key areas of your life. Activate any and all dreams whether practical or impractical. Have fun with this exercise and dig deep for the interests and goals that are in your heart. You are redefining what you want from your life enthusiastically reaching for your heart's desires.

Freely and vividly write down every thought that comes to mind. Paint the picture. In words, express how you would feel when you experience or accomplish what you are seeking. Link your values. Remember your hobbies. Ignite your passion, emotions and dreams.

Here are a few questions that I would like for you to consider as you brainstorm each key area of your life:

1. What do I want to experience or accomplish within a month, six months or year?
2. What do I want to experience or accomplish in the next 3-5 years?
3. What do I want to experience or accomplish in the next 10 years?

Step Three: Prioritize Your Goals

You've taken the time to think through what you want from your life. And that is so important. At times, the most challenging aspect of any worthwhile journey is getting started. It takes courage, commitment, and a change of thinking to take the path least traveled to reach your goals and milestones. A life filled with goals that you are passionate about is the journey worthy of consideration.

Prioritizing and setting goals give you a sense of direction and opportunity to channel your abilities, action needed, and resources. Passionate goals point you in the direction where you want to go and create a burning desire to focus. Feeling passionate about your goals drives you to succeed and achieve desired results. Achieving those results, gives you a sense of personal accomplishment.

Take a look at the brainstorming results of the six key areas of your life. Read through each brainstorm session and begin to think about prioritizing your goals. Ask yourself:

- Which experiences or goals do I value most and feel passionate about?
- What am I going to focus on right now?
- Am I ready to commit to myself by mustering and investing time, energy, or money in my desired experiences and goals without sacrificing my financial health and wellness?

From here, your next step is to write your goals in order of priority. Which goals and experiences do you want to begin working on right away? Which do you prefer to accomplish first? Second? Third? And so on.

Consider this. Write your goal in the positive tense rather than the negative. What I mean is you want to write your goal as if it is already achieved.

For example: Instead of writing your goal statement as "I want to get out of debt," say "I have a zero balance on my credit card accounts March 2011.

Can you feel the difference? Okay, now you try it. Place your goals under one of three categories:

- Short Term Goals: Experiences or goals that you would like to accomplish by the end of the month, six months, or year.
- Medium Term Goals: Experiences or goals that you want to achieve within one to five years.
- Long Term Goals: Experiences or goals that you want to accomplish 5, 10 or more years down the road.

Visualize achieving your goals as you are writing and tap into your feelings and passion. The more passionate and determined you are about achieving a goal, the likelihood of realizing your goal is greater.

Step Four: Design a Strategy for Living Life at Your Best

What's next? Design a strategy to accomplish what you want to experience and achieve. Create a plan for your life. Call it your life plan. Consider your life plan to be a road map that you can use as a guide to your experiences and goals. And should you find yourself distracted or off the course of your plan, your life plan will be resourceful to help you get back on the road again where you left off or lead you to another route to take.

You may be saying to yourself, "Where do I begin? I have a list of several goals in all areas of my life. On what should I focus my attention?" Well, it depends. It depends on what is most important to you? How busy are you? How well-balanced is your life right now? Are you strong and feeling fulfilled in some areas of your life and missing something in your life in other areas? The answers will highlight your priority areas and give you a good sense of where to begin shaping a well balanced lifestyle.

In a perfect world, a person who can balance carrying out experiences and goals effortlessly in each of the six key areas of life would be considered "a well rounded individual." Just know, this perfect world is imaginary. We are all a work in progress. Don't make perfect; make progress. You can bet that you will face challenges while working on your financial health and balancing your life. Nonetheless, expect challenges, overcome challenges and most of all learn from your challenges.

Speaking of challenges, challenge yourself to focus on goals in more than one key area of your life versus focusing your attention on many goals in just one area. I recommend choosing at least one short, medium and long term goal. It is perfectly fine to set more than one goal in multiple areas of your life as long as you are realistic about how many you can effectively pursue in a given time frame.

At the end of this financial fitness workout is a sample worksheet that you can use to map out a strategy for your life plan.

Follow along with me below as we:
- Define your goal.
- Identify resources that you will need or already have.
- Anticipate any obstacles or distractions in your way.
- Map a strategy for saving for financial goals.
- Map a strategy of action steps that you can take with targeted completion dates.

I am going walk you through your first goal. Then you get moving on the others. You will not need to be an architect to design a life plan. You do need to be a "thinker" so that you can think through the steps needed to accomplish your goal and a "go-getter" who takes action with focused intent.

Define Your Goal

On the worksheet below, define your goal and the area of your life you plan to fulfill. Then on the opposite page, write a goal statement in the positive tense as if it is already achieved.

Redefine and Design My Lifestyle
Area of My Life: _____
_____
_____
_____
_____
(examples: Financial, Career, Family etc.)

Redefine and Design My Lifestyle

My Goals:

_____

_____

_____

_____

_____

_____

_____

_____

_____

_____

_____

_____

_____

_____

_____

(examples)

I have a zero balance on my credit card account March 2011

I begin my career as a Web Developer April 2012.

I'm spending time with my parents for a week during the Christmas holiday this year.

Identify Resources

List any resources that you may already have that can be used to achieve your goal below. Also on the opposite page, list any resources that you may need. Spend ample time brainstorming about ways to muster resources. Ask yourself:

- What resources are necessary?
- How much time, energy and money will be needed?
- Do I have a lump sum of money that can be used to jump start a financial goal?
- Do I need to do some research?
- Will I need professional guidance, mentors, or other people's help?
- Will I need emotional support?

Resources

Resources That I Have:

Examples: – $50 dollars extra per month to put toward my credit card balances.
– My mentor.
– 5 hours a week that I can dedicate.

Chapter 1: What Comes First? Money or Lifestyle?

Resources

Resources That I Will Need:

_____
_____
_____
_____
_____
_____
_____
_____
_____
_____
_____
_____
_____
_____
_____
_____
_____
_____
_____
_____
_____
_____

Examples: – A part time job.
– A resume, personal references. etc.
– $200 for my parents Christmas gifts.

List Obstacles, Distractions, and Solutions

Obstacles come with the territory of any plan or goal. Always anticipate any obstacles that may have the potential to be a challenge followed up with a solution to overcome each. Sometimes right off hand you may know which obstacles or distractions you will face because they are either evident or have already been presented to you. Think about what can be done to remove the obstacles or distractions so that you can successfully "keep it moving" toward what you desire. And too, we can also be our own obstacle; we can get in our own way sometimes. Would you agree? Sometimes we need to try again, or just try harder, or learn from mistakes.

List your obstacles or distractions then list the solution to remove it.

Obstacles/Distractions	Solutions
1.	1.

Obstacles/Distractions	Solutions
2.	2.
3.	3.
4.	4.

Action Strategy Steps

Map out all of the action steps you will need to take to accomplish your goals within a realistic time frame. Consider aligning the steps in an order that you must follow to reach the goal. Be clear about which step comes first. Which is second? And so on. Create a list of as many steps necessary.

Financial Strategy Steps

If money is a resource for your goal and requires regularly saving, what is the total amount needed for your goal? How much can you save each week or month toward the goal? How many weeks, months, or years will it take to accomplish your savings goal? Do the math and record it on your goal sheet.

Target a Date for Completion

Hold yourself accountable by setting targeted completion dates for each step. Set mini benchmarks that add up. Each step will give you the momentum that will propel you to continue moving toward achieving your goals.

A Strategy of Steps For My Goal	Target Completion Date
_____	_____
_____	
_____	
_____	

A Strategy of Steps For My Goal	Target Completion Date
_____ _____ _____ _____ _____	_____
_____ _____ _____ _____ _____	_____
_____ _____ _____ _____ _____	_____
Examples: – Put $20 in an envelope in my dresser drawer, each pay period, over the next 10 weeks to finance my Mom and Dad's Christmas gift.	Oct. 10, 2009

Step 5: Feel Inspired to Take Definite Action

You will feel inspired when you are investing time, energy, and money on what matters most to you.

Okay now take the plunge...experience your first steps, mark it completed, and take another. As you successfully make inroads on your life plan your confidence, commitment and motivation will snowball in your favor. There is a sweet sensation when you build momentum toward accomplishing anything worthwhile.

Try your best to be patient and flexible as you progress toward your goals. In light of what you experience while on your journey, you may find that you need to adjust or revise your strategy and time lines. Be open to making necessary positive changes along the way.

Most of all don't lose sight of your values. Your values are the silver lining of your life and basis of your actions and decisions. Allow your values to lead you and influence the way you approach and execute your life. We live by our values and become what we value.

Your 60 Second Cooling Period

Lifestyle first, then money.

Young people you are destined for financial freedom. But you got to want it. I will admit that it takes time to change your life for the better financially and there will be some work to be done on your part. Always remember, a financial fitness lifestyle is a journey. You will get better at it over time.

Going forward, see yourself as the CEO of your life. After all, you really are. Your lifestyle is your business. I mean that literally. What happens to a business that does not have a business plan or a clearly defined focus on business goals? And what if the business takes on excessive debt, blindly spends money, and fails to improve resources and chances for success? The answers are it is possible the business will not grow or may become a candidate for bankruptcy or may no longer operate and close its doors. How would you feel if that happened to your lifestyle? It will not feel good. I know it. Follow the advice on personal money management in the next upcoming chapters to ensure that you will create a sustainable flourishing style of living that you will enjoy.

Design My Best Lifestyle

Area of My Life:

My Goal:

Resources

Resources That I Have	Resources That I Will Need
1	1
2	2
3	3
4	4

Obstacles/Distractions	Solutions
1	1
2	2
3	3

Strategy of Steps For My Goals	Target Completion Date
1	1
2	2
3	3
4	4
5	5

CHAPTER 2

PLANS FOR SPENDING

A night out on the town with friends Ka-Ching! A Latte everyday Ka-Ching! $10 lunches with co-workers Ka-Ching! Car repairs, rent, mortgage, cell phone bills, Ka-Ching! Ka-Ching! Ka-Ching! Expected or unexpected spending must go on!

Many people spend money without an awareness of their financial reality. They are not aware of exactly how much income flows into their household on a monthly basis or how much money it takes to keep their lifestyle intact each month. Nor do they know how much money is supposed to be left over after paying monthly bills.

If you have a vague idea of how much money is coming into your household or where your money is going, you cannot make conscious decisions about investing your money in what matters most to you. You need to know the answers to your financial reality:

- How much money is needed to sustain your lifestyle every month without fail?
- How much money is actually coming into your household monthly?

- How much money is needed to fund your goals?
- What are you planning to spend money on today, this week, this month, this year?

In order to effectively finance your lifestyle, you must have an awareness of your financial reality and a plan for spending your money. The old school called this being on a budget. On the contrary, budgets are not successful. Why? It is because the word budget has a negative connotation and is stifling. When the concept "budgeting" was created, it was designed to curb spending, restrict you from putting money on what is suppose to be things "all people can live without" or better yet penny pinching and save the rest. No fun allowed! Essentially, budgeting took away the freedom to spend your money on anything outside of the household expenses. Most people run in the opposite direction of any budget that will force spending restrictions.

A favorable less restrictive way to get familiar with your financial reality is to create a spending plan. A spending plan is a tool that gives you the freedom to plan and make choices about how you will spend your money. A spending plan opens up your awareness of your financial reality and helps you customize a balanced approach to spending by allocating money across various areas of your lifestyle that matter most to you. An effective spending plan mirrors your lifestyle and includes savings for your financial security, every day living expenses, your life plan goals and other lifestyle activities too.

In order to design a spending plan that mirrors your lifestyle and follow it effectively, you must have a clear idea of what your lifestyle looks like today, what it will cost to sustain it, as well as how much money is required to save for your future goals or expand your lifestyle. In the previous chapter, you identified your values, goals and plans for expanding your life. Your next step is to get in tuned with your money and align it with your life plans so that it is being spent in the right places for your ideal lifestyle. A spending plan tool can help you point your money in the right direction.

> **CHANGE YOUR LIFE FOR THE BETTER FINANCIALLY**
>
> **Simple Step #2:
> Design a Spending Plan
> That Mirrors Your Lifestyle**

A New World of Financial Responsibility

Do you remember your first job and how much you were paid regularly? Do you recall having ideas and plans for your weekly paycheck? It probably felt great also to not be somewhat dependent on your parents financially, right? Do you remember the first time when your parents allowed you to have financial responsibility for something? Maybe it was paying for a portion of the car insurance when you became a driver, the car's maintenance or your telephone bill? Nonetheless, you began to experience what it would be like to have a paycheck and a regular monthly bill for the first time. Then as time moved on and you became more and more independent, you added additional financial responsibility to your plate. Could it have been college expenses, or rent and utilities? The real life expenses started kicking in one at time slowly but surely. Or maybe not so slowly! It can be overwhelming trying to keep up with the constant expansion and evolution of your lifestyle, especially if you are not aware of your financial reality.

You can expect the constant expansion of financial responsibility to continue as you continually expand your lifestyle. Overwhelmingly, your finances can spin out of control if you are not careful with the way you handle your money while maintaining or expanding your life's needs and goals. If you are a young adult who has married and started a family, I am sure you can relate. Likewise if you are a young adult who has stepped out on your own after high school or college to a whole new world of financial responsibility, you can certainly relate.

Without a spending plan, which can help you gain control of your money, your financial reality will become unfamiliar to you. You will find yourself feeling your money being pulled from you in different directions like a juggling act because you are not making conscious choices about how your money should be spent. The sooner you begin to use a spending plan tool and get a hold of your money the more nimble you can be when planning spending for your expected or unexpected lifestyle expenses. Also, you will have more confidence in your ability to sustain and expand your lifestyle because you can be realistic about it.

A Practical Balanced Approach to Your Spending Plan

Creating a spending plan to map out a realistic, balanced way to spend your money before it leaves your bank account is the easy part. The challenge is following your spending plan without wavering in your commitment to spend your money in areas of your

Chapter 2: Plans for Spending

lifestyle that support your life plans and goals. Why is that such a challenge? Distractions in your life can throw you off track from focusing on what is important to you. Advertisements and competition for your money in the market place can entice you to spend money on things that are not on your list of goals and plans leaving you unsure of where your money went. Additionally, falling for the trappings of a borrowed lifestyle by using credit cards and succumbing to instant gratification ties up your future income and detracts your money from opportunities to accomplish your goals and build wealth.

However, I promise you will be able to overcome any challenge proposed to your spending plan if you faithfully practice the following practical advice every pay period month after month.

1. Focus on what you want in life.
2. Put money into your financial freedom fund first.
3. Consciously live within your means.
4. Use cash vs. credit cards.

Focus On What You Want In Life

If you lose focus on what you want to accomplish in your life you can easily lose direction for your life and your money. With no intentional direction for your life, it is possible your lifetime and money can fritter away leaving you unfulfilled without accomplishing anything and frustrated financially. But you can avoid this from happening to you if you keep your mind on your spending plan and align it with your life plan. Plus, by aligning your time, energy and money with your goals in life, you will be able to identify and eliminate any challenge of a distracting nature that does not coincide with what matters most to you, including poor spending habits.

As you move through life you will face challenges and unexpected changes that are good for you or not so good. When you do, always bring yourself back to the drawing board and rework your plans; rearrange your life plans and spending plan to accommodate your immediate changes. Always have a plan mapped out for your lifestyle and money. They are your road maps to help keep you focused on what is important to you and how to spend your money accordingly. Make your time, energy and money work for benefit always. Once you lose it, you cannot get it back. You will have to make up for it.

Put Money Into Your Financial Freedom Fund First

A powerful effective strategy for building wealth is to open up an investment savings vehicle and "pay yourself" first before spending money on anything else. Label this account your financial freedom fund. Saving money plays a major role in your financial future. Paying yourself first on a regular monthly basis helps you build a financial freedom fund that gets you closer and closer to a lifestyle with no financial barriers.

The opposite of paying yourself first is to spend it all first and see what happens. And what happens? You may not have enough money that will give you the confidence to take charge when an emergency arises, or take advantage of opportunities that can expand your lifestyle. Worst case scenario you may need to continue working beyond retirement age.

The best kept secret to the game of wealth accumulation for long term financial security is not so much the dollar amount you pay yourself first and invest along the way, but the consistency with time and persistence with which you are doing it. Money can grow over time and accumulate wealth just by saving and investing in a modest fashion on a regular basis. Take a look at the chart below.

THE POWER OF PAYING YOURSELF FIRST CREATES WEALTH

Annual Rate of Compound Interest

	5%	7%	10%
$100/month			
5 Years	$6,809	$7,160	$7,717
10 Years	$15,499	$17,202	$20,146
20 Years	$40,746	$51,041	$72,399
30 Years	$81,870	$117,606	$207,929
$250/month			
5 Years	$17,023	$17,900	$19,293
10 Years	$38,748	$43,005	$50,364
20 Years	$101,864	$127,602	$180,997
30 years	$204,674	$294,016	$519,823
$500/month			
5 Years	$34,045	$35,799	$38,586
10 Years	$77,496	$86,009	$100,729
20 Years	$203,729	$255,203	$361,993
30 Years	$409,349	$588,032	$1,039,646

There are various types of financial vehicles that can help you build wealth. A financial advisor can help you make informed choices about saving and investing in your financial future. The above example does not take taxes into consideration, nor does it include any fees or expenses usually associated with the purchase of a financial vehicle.

Young adults have the greatest advantage to accumulate wealth and build financial freedom because you have time on your side. Your young age affords you the time to accumulate wealth modestly by saving $100-$500 each month over 20-40 years. You can potentially set yourself up for a lifestyle with no financial barriers; that is if you want financial freedom.

What if you were taught in high school:

Once you become an adult and begin earning an income to support your lifestyle, before deciding what kind of car, apartment, or home you are going to finance, before deciding how much money you are going to spend on any other lifestyle expense or fun, decide how much money you are going to put away every month until you achieve financial freedom. Each month, would you invest and sock away $100, $250, $500 or more? Well how much you'd put on financial freedom would depend on how soon you wanted to be free financially right? You got to want it to get it.

Suppose your were introduced to financial freedom and how to achieve it were clearly defined when you were in high school and it was then when you visualized what your lifestyle would look like with no financial barriers. Do you think you may have started your independent lifestyle differently? Do you think young people would be compelled to build wealth versus compete for who has the best looking car, clothes, shoes, material stuff, and so on? Perhaps we would have more young people bragging about how close they are to financial freedom versus how close they are to the mall to get some bling.

Is spending your life's time with no financial barriers important to you? Isn't now a good time to approach your independent lifestyle differently? You may need to change your spending behavior in

Chapter 2: Plans for Spending

order to accomplish this or eliminate expenses that can be traded in for financial freedom. Are you willing to do that and change your life for the better financially?

Can you commit to approach your spending plan each month starting with deciding how much of your monthly take home pay will be saved or invested regularly to secure long term financial security? Consider this. Pay yourself first and incorporate monthly savings directed to a financial freedom fund into your spending plan just as you would include rent, mortgage, or a car note. The longer you persist paying yourself first, wealth modestly builds naturally. Meet with a financial professional to discuss the best financial savings vehicle for your financial freedom fund.

Consciously Living Within Your Means

It takes a conscious effort to live within your means and be in tuned with your money at all times. The basic idea of living within your means is to squarely face how much money you have coming into your household on a monthly basis and make plans for your lifestyle accordingly. Ultimately, you want to honor your spending plan without over spending your monthly take home pay or borrowing from next month's pay check and credit cards. Believe it or not many people are not sure if they are living within their means. In many cases they may fall under one of the following categories:

1. Either you know you make more than enough money necessary for your lifestyle and so you spend freely versus being more effective with your money. Just know, money is leaking from your wallet that can be directed toward lifestyle goals that offer fulfillment in different areas of your life and/or building financial freedom at an advantageous pace.

2. Or, you just can't ever get a handle on your money. You pay for everyday living expenses with credit cards because you never seem to have enough money to do all the things you want to do. In this case you may be living beyond your means because you view credit cards as an additional source of income. If you continue living this way, your lifestyle will be at a dead end and loaded with debt until you design a spending plan that realistically reflects what you can afford. From there, you can sensibly approach how to increase your income so that you can expand your lifestyle comfortably without sacrificing your financial well being.

Getting into the habit of living within your financial reality and revisiting your spending plan every pay period effectively helps you build your lifestyle. There is a meaningful reason why you planned for your money to go toward certain areas of your life, according to a plan. Ideally, this conscious reasoning supports the experiences, goals and financial security you desire.

Use Cash vs. Credit Cards

There is a fine line between paying wisely and spending above your means. Always know it is better to forego purchases until you can afford to pay for them in cash rather than to borrow from future income using credit cards to satisfy "instantly wanting" something now. It is no secret credit card debt negatively impacts your financial health. Nine times out of ten, people use credit cards to buy things they cannot afford or do not "need." If you are using credit cards to buy things you cannot afford, you are spending above your means and living a borrowed lifestyle.

Chapter 2: Plans for Spending

Credit card offers are disguised to be a convenient benefit. But who is benefiting? Credit card companies estimate consumers spend 2-3 times more when paying with a credit card versus cash, check or check card. It is no wonder every retailer has their very own store branded credit card. Retailers are convincing you to spend above your means, plus make money on the credit card's high interest rates you are paying. To sweeten the deal, they create advertising and sales pitches to influence your spending behavior. I know you heard this one, "Open a charge account today and save 10% on your purchase" when in fact credit cards just aren't a good influence on your personal finances. However, it comes down to this; it is your responsibility to walk away from a bad influence.

So often you are tempted by crafty credit card advertising to spend beyond your means and go into debt when it is not even necessary. It seems like the convenience of using credit cards makes it a little too easy to spend money. Let's be honest. Just about any place consumers shop, there is an option to pay with credit. And now you know why. Even fast food restaurants have joined the line up! But you must exercise caution. Use good, old fashion cash instead of whipping out the plastic and not worrying whether or not you have the money. For if you don't exercise caution there is a trade off. And that is, borrow money for things you cannot afford today and in the future money is tied up making credit card payments and so are you. You traded in your financial freedom for sales and thrills.

Imagine having $10,000 in your savings account, $25,000 in a mutual fund, or $100,000 in your 401k. How would that feel? That is a good start and a good phase one goal for financial freedom. It is not impossible to achieve when you make the decision to make smart choices about your money, pay yourself first, live within your means, and pay wisely with cash. Modestly saving $250 per month instead of making what may seem like a never ending $250 per month payment toward credit cards is the trade off that can pay off for you.

> ## Your Financial Fitness Workout:
> ### Design A Spending Plan That Mirrors Your Lifestyle

During this workout, I will coach you on how to design an effective spending plan. As you move through the exercise, keep in mind a spending plan is not meant to be restrictive or inflexible. Nor should your approach to a spending plan be to reduce spending unless you are living beyond your means, or not saving for your goals and financial freedom.

Your objective is to create a spending plan that gives you the freedom to plan a balanced lifestyle and make conscious decisions about what is reasonable to save, invest, and spend in each area of your life. When you decide ahead of time how your money will be put to good use, you gain control of your money and there is a tremendous chance that you will accomplish your goals, build wealth and live comfortably.

This financial workout will challenge you to:

- Find money that is leaking from your wallet.
- Pay yourself first.
- Know how much money it takes to sustain your lifestyle.

- Create an effective spending plan designed for a balanced lifestyle.

Step One: Track Your Daily Spending

Your first steps to creating a spending plan is tracking your daily spending, getting a grasp of your spending habits both good and bad, and finding money that may be leaking from your wallet. The purpose of this exercise is to regain consciousness of where your money is going and recapture dollars leaking from your wallet that you can put to better use. After all, before you are able to control your money, you will need to know what to control. Could it be impulsive shopping, using credit cards instead of cash, pulling money out of the ATM and not knowing where the money went, or you just can't seem to pass up the coffee house and buying a latte along with a pastry every morning. It is easy to spot when the big money may be leaving your wallet and could be better served. However, it is the little money leaking that adds up quickly and goes unnoticed such as work lunches, take out and fast food.

There are three simple steps to track spending:

1. Each day write down what you spend your money on.
2. At the end of each week, add the total for weekly spending.
3. At the end of the month, add the total for monthly spending.

Over the next month, on a weekly basis, track everything you spend money on by writing it down. Get yourself a small memo pad and when you make a purchase just pull it out and jot what you bought and how much the item cost. Write down every purchase from a soda to a movie ticket. Include payments for your regular bills like rent, mortgage, cable etc. Leave no purchase behind. Each time you make a purchase keep your life plan in mind and ask yourself:

- Is this purchase necessary? Is this a need or want?
- Is this purchase in support of my goals and ideal lifestyle or taking money away from it?
- Am I spending within my means?

Each week tally the total amount of money you've spent and take special notice of the types of items you've bought. Do this for at least 4 weeks. Then tally the total you spent for the month. You may be surprised at the difference between how you think money is being spent and what the actual items and cost turn out to be. For example, you may realize you spent $250 dining out that month which turned out to be more than you spent on groceries, or that you can be impulsive when shopping.

Make this exercise a fun way to gain insight into your spending habits - good or bad. Most of all get tuned in with your money. Know when money is coming into your possession, when it is leaving, where it is going and why. You can really make it fun by getting your family and friends on board with achieving financial freedom. Together you can be one another's cheerleader and sounding board for financial fitness discussions. Make it a plan to track your expenses together each week; then have a discussion about how your week went. Talk about your spending behavior and spending habits that can be changed or tweaked. And most importantly discuss what went well for you. Help each other make a change for the better financially.

Side Note:

Beginning with the next upcoming Sunday start your first week. Continue your financial fitness reading and move on to the next chapters while tracking your expenses over the next 4 weeks. When you are done with the daily tracking, return to this chapter and begin Step 2: Design a Monthly Spending Plan That Mirrors Your Lifestyle.

Step 2: Design a Monthly Spending Plan That Mirrors Your Lifestyle

Now that you are aware of your spending patterns and habits, it is a good time to design your spending plan. What did you learn about your spending during the daily expense tracking exercise? Did you become more mindful of when money left your wallet and for what purpose? Were you able to recognize expenses that were not related to your goals or lifestyle plans? Do have you any expenses where spending can be reduced or eliminated so that you can free up money that can be used to pay yourself first or fund a goal? You also may have identified ways to transform bad spending habits into wealth building opportunities. Every dollar counts.

The expense tracking exercise is a good way to help bring back to focus what is or is not necessary to include in your spending plan. Continue tracking your expenses for the next 60-90 days to really hone in on your spending patterns and getting in tuned with your money. Each month bring what you learned to the table when you sit down and revisit your spending plan each pay day.

Next, design a spending plan with a practical balanced approach to spending. Seize your freedom to make conscious choices about what is reasonable to spend in every area of your life. You can begin designing your spending plan using a sheet of paper or you may find an alternative like Excel or personal finance software like Quicken, Microsoft Money, etc suitable for your personality. It does not matter what method you use to design your spending plan as long as it helps you actively manage and control your money.

On a sheet of paper or other spending plan tool approach, design your spending plan in this order:

1. **List income sources:** list sources of income and take home pay that you know for sure is coming into your household. Then calculate the total.

    This is your financial reality, your means. Next, design your spending plan within you means.

2. **Pay yourself first:** Identify how much you will invest in your financial freedom fund each month.

3. **List the unique expenses of your lifestyle:** Now is the time to tailor your spending plan so that it reflects your lifestyle. Spread your money across different areas of your lifestyle. Include line items for savings goals dedicated to your future life plans. Take into account the six key areas of your life:
    - Career/Professional
    - Community
    - Family/Relationships
    - Financial
    - Personal
    - Spiritual

Chapter 2: Plans for Spending						45

On the pages 46-47, there is a listing of typical lifestyle expenses. I've included this listing to help you identify or begin thinking of expenses that mirror your lifestyle needs.

Now go to work and have fun designing your spending plan. It is all about you, your financial freedom, basic living expenses, lifestyle experiences and goals.

Design your monthly spending without forgetting about any quarterly, semi-annual or annual expenses that can catch you by surprise when the bill is due. I am referring to expenses like car insurance, life insurance premiums, property taxes, tuition etc. Build into your spending plan monthly savings for expenses like these scheduled to be paid varying times throughout the year. This way you won't be caught off guard when it is time to make the payment because you saved up for it over time.

I cannot promise following your new spending plan will be effortless when you begin. However, your new spending plan is designed with so much meaning and thought about what is important to you. How can you not commit to improve your chances to change your life for the better financially and live at your best? You will get better and better at it as you consciously plan, spend and focus on what matters most to you.

Your last step in planning your spending is to crunch the numbers to see where you stand. Add up your financial freedom fund and lifestyle expenses then subtract the total from your available monthly income. Are you within your means? Or are you over the mark?

Household Expenses		Liabilities Monthly Payment	
Rent/Mortgage		Credit Card	
Condo/Neighborhood Assoc. fees		Student Loan	
Utilities/Gas/Electric		Home Equity Loan or Line of Credit	
Telephone		Auto Loan or Lease	
Cell Phone/PDA		Other monthly bills	
Cable TV/Satellite Dish		**Children's Expenses**	
TIVO		Child Support	
High Speed Internet/ Wireless Internet		Nanny	
Groceries		School tuition	
Housekeeper		Daycare	
Landscaping		Babysitter	
Auto Maintenance/Oil Changes		Weekly Allowance	
Gasoline		School supplies	
Insurance Portfolio		After school activities, lessons, sports	
Life Insurance		Braces	
Disability Insurance		Clothing, Uniforms	
Auto Insurance		Birthday Party	
Renters/Homeowners		**Personal Care**	
Umbrella Insurance		Hair Care	
Health Insurance (individual policy only)		Manicure, Pedicure	
Medical Expenses		Massages	
Co-pays/Doctor/Dentist		Cosmetics, Skin Care	
Prescriptions		Facials	
Out of pocket health care costs		Health & Fitness Membership	
Deductible		Spa	
Over the counter vitamins, medications		Clothing	

Chapter 2: Plans for Spending

Travel and Entertainment		Charitable Contributions	
Dining Out		Church tithes	
Movie Theater		Donations	
Plays, Concerts, Museums		**Hobbies**	
Sporting Events		Golf Fees	
After work Cocktails		Tennis	
Networking Events		Sporting Equipment	
Dinner Parties		Sporting Apparel	
Weekend Getaways		Books	
Conferences		Magazines	
Hotel		Music CD's	
Flights		IPod Downloads	
Rental Car		Computer Downloads	
DVD Rentals		Computer Subscriptions	
Netflix, Blockbuster fees		Satellite Radio Subscription	
Wine Club		Video Games	
Alcoholic Beverages for Home		Other Hobby	
Your Monthly Allowance		**Other Annual Expenses**	
Work Lunches		Vacation	
Snacks		Vacation Spending $	
Coffee		Professional Dues	
Cigars, Cigarettes		Property Taxes	
Pocket Money		Club Dues	
Unplanned Expenses		**Pets**	
Gifts To Others		Pet Insurance, Vet fees	
Weddings		Pet Food	
Birthdays		Groomer, Dog Walker	
Anniversaries		Medicine, heartworms, fleas, ticks	
Christmas Holiday			

If you come up with a number in the red, don't get discouraged. Chances are you can make some exceptions or change your spending levels in areas where you can be flexible. Just think, it is better to know your financial reality and see it as a positive motivator to seek ways to increase your income so that you can begin to expand your lifestyle. Nonetheless give yourself a new healthy beginning to a financial fitness lifestyle and plan within your means. You can grow from here.

If your spending plan came in below your means, before money leaks from your wallet, consider directing your extra money toward a balanced combination of:

- Increasing your monthly savings and investments.
- Funding a new personal goal.
- Exploring opportunities to expand your lifestyle's activities.

The bottom line is to get a good hold of your extra money so that you will know where it is going and have something to show for your hard earned cash.

Step 3: Plan Your Spending Each Pay Day

Each pay period take an active role in managing your personal finances. Re-visit your spending plan and decide which expenses are to be covered by your pay check. This is a profound spending habit to adopt and use whenever you receive income, bonuses, or a windfall of money. If you do this, you won't throw your money away. You will plan your money in ways that serve the purpose of living life at your best and building financial freedom.

Your 60 Second Cooling Period

Poor spending habits can be broken and changed for the better. You can change your life for the better financially beginning right now by aligning your time, energy and money with your values and purpose.

By now, your money consciousness level has increased. You are consciously aware of when money is in your bank account, wallet, in your possession, when it leaves, and why. Go a step further. Stretch your awareness to consciously build wealth over time using your hard earned money one dollar at a time. Aren't you worthy?

CHAPTER 3

Financial Wealth Check

Annual check ups are not reserved for physical health and fitness alone. Maintaining your financial health and wealth building momentum requires, at a minimum, an annual financial check up too. A significant examination of your financial health and measurement of your wealth building progress is performed by monitoring your net worth year after year.

Tell me. Think quickly. What is your net worth? Most people can quickly recite their annual salary, or what they "think" their home or 401k is worth. When it comes to knowing their net worth, the same people are puzzled, not sure. If you are not sure of your net worth, it is fair to say, you are not sure about the true state of your financial health. It is also fair to reason you may not be sure you are building wealth year after year. How will you really know if you are making healthy financial choices and getting ahead financially? The answer is giving yourself a financial checkup by creating, monitoring and updating your net worth statement on a yearly basis.

Your net worth is the sum of your assets, what you own, minus the sum of your liabilities, what you owe. It represents the value of your actual accumulated wealth.

Chapter 3: Financial Wealth Check

A net worth statement is a universal tool that is used to tally your net worth by itemizing your assets and liabilities. Drafting a net worth statement is simple and easy. Just simply list your assets, their values, and total in one column. In a separate column, do the same for your liabilities by listing your debt and the outstanding balances. Take a look at the example of a net worth statement on the below.

ASSETS		LIABILITIES	
Savings	$5,000	Credit Card #1	$3,500
Checking	$0	Credit Card #2	$0
CD's	$3,000	Credit Card #3	$0
Bonds	$0	Student Loan	$40,000
Mutual Funds	$6,000	Mortgage	$250,000
Stock	$0	Home Equity Loan	$0
Real Estate	305,000	Auto Loan	$27,000
IRA's	$9,000	Line of Credit	$0
401k/Other Retirement Plans	$18,000	Personal Loan	$0
Cash Value of Life Insurance	$1,000	Medical Bills	$0
Jewelry	$10,000	Unpaid Taxes	$0
Antiques/Collectibles	$0		
Art	$2,000		
Auto	$25,000		
Total Assets	$384,000	Total Liabilities	$320,500
Net Worth $63,500			

As simple as the net worth statement may seem at a glance, the major role it plays in gauging the status of your financial health and wealth building progress cannot be discounted. Just like a spending plan can help you analyze what you are spending your money on and direct money toward what matters most to you; a net worth statement helps you analyze how you are using your money to build financially. Net worth statements do not measure your cash flow but there is a clear relationship between how you spend, save, or invest your money and what your financial picture looks like.

Basically your net worth statement reveals what you have to show for your hard earned dollars. For example, does your financial picture reveal advancement toward financial goals? Is your financial health bleeding because of excessive debt? Are you accumulating or depleting assets? Or do you have a balanced savings and investment strategy representing an emergency fund, a financial freedom fund, and a fund for your goals?

There also exists a clear relationship between your self esteem and your net worth. You may ask, what does self esteem have to do with it? Everything. Self esteem influences your priorities, what you value focusing on, your active role and direction in life. For instance, are you going forward financially, backwards, or are you paralyzed in place? No matter which direction you are heading rest assured your self esteem has everything to do with it. High or low self esteem reflects your actions and attitude toward your worthiness to experience a fulfilling life, maintaining a clean bill of financial health and willingness to build wealth. Self esteem can make or break your success with anything in life including changing your life for the better financially.

Chapter 3: Financial Wealth Check

There are endeavors that young adults aspire to accomplish with great confidence and high self esteem such as researching, planning and pursuing a career. In planning a career, you are likely to conduct due diligence and create a checklist of systematic steps for a career path. Once a plan is in place and your heart is set on pursuing options to fulfill your career goals, you'll confidently hit the trail to do whatever it takes to become a candidate for your chosen occupation. Because after all, your lifestyle is dependent upon you being actively employed and supporting it financially.

As young adults, you must pursue your goal to get financially fit and achieve financial freedom in your lifetime with the same self assurance and tenacity as any endeavor you confidently pursue. Frankly speaking, you have no choice but to provide for your financial well being. Money is the biggest worry of most people. They worry about not having enough money, worry about being in debt, going bankrupt, worry about sending their children to college and about their retirement. When the economy takes a downturn or people experience a loss in income, they worry about surviving period. Don't let that be you. No one wants to live life constantly worrying about money. Yet, many people lack the confidence to make changes to improve their financial situation so that they can have financial security and peace of mind. Your financial security and future is depending on you and your active role.

Achieving any goal in life is a personal choice. It just doesn't happen without a desire or effort. You can decide today that you are going to make healthy financial choices, spend time, energy and money responsibly and increase your financial security so that you don't have to worry about money. Young adults, it is possible for you to build wealth modestly and increase your net worth year after year if you "choose" to do so. It may require learning more about personal finance and how to invest; therefore you must conduct due diligence and seek information. It may require a check list of steps to take to get your financial health in order or a meeting with a financial professional to get direction on how to begin. For certain, it requires your active participation including giving yourself an annual financial check up to monitor your wealth building momentum every year.

> **CHANGE YOUR LIFE FOR THE BETTER FINANCIALLY**
>
> **Simple Step #3:
> Increase Your Net Worth
> Year After Year**

How to Increase Your Net Worth

Increasing your net worth on an annual basis is not out of reach for young adults who are patient, use debt wisely, and carve a wealth building expenditure into a monthly spending plan. An opportunity to build wealth is not about how much money you earn but about how much you keep from your income every month.

There is no fast track to wealth; wealth must be accumulated slowly and consistently with an all encompassing approach in mind.

An encompassing approach integrates:
- The wealth building sweet spot
- Using debt minimally
- Learning how to invest

The Wealth Building Sweet Spot

The practical way to build wealth is to spend less and invest more. Invest more by simply carving into your spending plan a monthly wealth building expenditure that is up to 10% of your income. Investing 10% of your income each month is the plateau which I call the wealth building sweet spot. Are you there yet? If you are not currently investing each month at this rate while experiencing a fun balanced lifestyle, simply consider working toward combining your readiness, discipline and a healthy objection to the tide of material consumption so that you can find your sweet spot over the next 1-3 years. As you get closer and closer to your sweet spot your wealth building momentum builds, and builds. When you reach your sweet spot stay the course and become accustomed to not missing the money you are investing.

Creating wealth building momentum and striving to reach your wealth building sweet spot doesn't mean deprive yourself or become pennywise. Absolutely design a spending plan based on what you need and carve out some money toward investing, fun and entertainment. What you choose to spend money on for you and your family may involve personal decisions. However, what you want to avoid is squandering your money through carelessness, impulsiveness, or keeping up appearances. The careless dollars spent can add up to a pretty penny each month that can be allocated for your wealth building sweet spot.

For example: If your annual income is $60,000. Over time, strive to get to the 10% savings mark, $6,000 per year. Divided over twelve months that equals $500 per month. See my favorite chart below that illustrates how your money may grow and compound interest.

The Power of Compounding Interest			
	5%	7%	10%
$100/month			
5 Years	$6,809	$7,160	$7,717
10 Years	$15,499	$17,202	$20,146
20 Years	$40,746	$51,041	$72,399
30 Years	$81,870	$117,606	$207,929
$250/month			
5 Years	$17,023	$17,900	$19,293
10 Years	$38,748	$43,005	$50,364
20 Years	$101,864	$127,602	$180,997
30 years	$204,674	$294,016	$519,823
$500/month			
5 Years	$34,045	$35,799	$38,586
10 Years	$77,496	$86,009	$100,729
20 Years	$203,729	$255,203	$361,993
30 Years	$409,349	$588,032	$1,039,646

There are various types of financial vehicles that can help you build wealth. A financial advisor can help you make informed choices about saving and investing in your financial future. The above example does not take taxes into consideration, nor does it include any fees or expenses usually associated with the purchase of a financial vehicle.

Fast forward to the future. You are 30 years older; you've invested $500 per month for 30 years averaging a 10% rate of return. You now have a total investment of $1,039,646. What do you do next? Could it be you have achieved financial freedom? My answer is maybe. It depends on your annual lifestyle expenses. Your lifestyle expenses set the bar you need to hurdle for financial freedom. Your annual expenses determine how much wealth you'll need to generate a reliable annual income stream sufficient for your lifestyle indefinitely. You don't have to be a certain age or have a certain amount of money to achieve financial freedom. You arrive at financial freedom when your investment account balance can produce a perpetual annual income for your lifestyle expenses that you cannot outlive.

> For example: By making a 5% annual withdrawal from an account balance of $1,039,646 earning an average 10% each year, you can generate an investment income of $51,982. If your lifestyle expenses meet or are below $51,982, you achieved financial freedom. Does that make sense?
>
> Young adults, consciously make money work for you not against you. Consider developing a new attitude "I'm frugal for financial freedom." Your new attitude and self esteem will steer you to do more with less money. You may find yourself cutting back on the little luxuries, passing up buying items with credit cards and saving for large purchases. If you do this, you can find money that can be invested in a positive financial direction.

Using Debt Minimally

You noticed on the net worth statement at the beginning of this chapter that debt cancels wealth. There are different types of debt, most of them bad but some actually good for you.

Types of bad debt. Bad debt is considered bad and unwise because it is used to enhance lifestyles in frivolous ways such as buying material things as opposed to enhancing financial security or your net worth. Making monthly payments on bad debt takes away from your opportunity to put money toward your wealth building sweet spot.

High interest debt: Paying high interest is not a good financial strategy. Ridiculously high interest rates force you to pay far more money for the goods and services that you are purchasing. What can help curtail high interest debt is having a strong credit score that entitles you to low interest rates when borrowing.

Auto debt: Your car is not an investment. It is a depreciating asset that decreases your net worth over time. Auto financing is an expense. You have an opportunity to practice your new attitude "I'm frugal for financial freedom" in this area and make practical decisions when seeking financing options for a car. Rather than having a fancy car note of $550 or more per month. Consider a vehicle you can get into for $250-$400 per month at the lowest possible interest rate and invest the difference. An extra $100-$200 per month in an investment plan can build more wealth for you than the vehicle you decide to drive.

Types of good debt. Leveraging good debt in moderation is key to financial success.

> **Mortgage:** A mortgage loan leverages the purchase of real estate which may increase in value and enhance your wealth. Homeownership is financially productive because historically real estate by far is the single greatest investment opportunity. As real estate increases in value and your mortgage loan balance declines your net worth increases.
>
> **Student loans:** Leveraging student loans to invest in an education that yields a rewarding salary is considered a good use of debt. If you are a college student or planning to attend, plan ahead and calculate how much you may need to finance your college expenses and what your student loan monthly repayments will be in the future. Then research the starting income in the current marketplace for your chosen occupation. A good rule of thumb is to plan and borrow wisely ensuring student loan payments won't exceed seven percent of your anticipated first-year monthly income after graduation.

Good debt can be self destructive if you finance more house than you can reasonably afford or if you have too many investment properties than you can financially handle. The same consequence holds true for taking on too much in student loans as compared to your anticipated starting salary upon graduation.

Learn How To Invest

Learn investment basics and become a "disciplined" investor who increases his or her net worth every year. A disciplined investor invests money to build wealth on a consistent basis and also has a fundamental understanding of investment vehicles such as stocks, bonds, mutual funds and the risk involved when investing. The essential investment basics you need to know to become a disciplined investor are:

#1: Risk vs. Reward

#2: Types of investment vehicles

#3: Types of investment accounts

#4: How to choose and partner with a financial professional

Risk vs. Reward

Investment vehicles can be a resource to take you to the destination financial freedom. There are varying types of vehicles such as stocks, bonds, and mutual funds to help you get there. Each investment vehicle bears a relationship between risk and reward. Risk is inherent in investing. The greater the potential for the highest interest rate or return on the investment the higher the risk of losing the value of your investment. Before choosing an investment vehicle for your wealth building strategy, gain a fundamental understanding of the investment's risk factor vs. the potential losses or reward. Always know what the downside or upside potential exists in the investment vehicle.

Types of Investment Vehicles

Stocks. When investing in stock of a publicly traded company on a stock exchange you become a shareholder of the corporation. There are two types of stock that you may consider as an investment: common and preferred. As a shareholder of common stock you are entitled to attend annual meetings and vote on important decisions that relate to the direction and management of the company. Preferred stock shareholders have restricted or no voting rights; however they are entitled to a benefit not offered to common stock shareholders, a guaranteed fixed payable dividend. Dividends are additional profits paid to preferred stock shareholders and can be withdrawn from the investment account as investment income the year received or reinvested to buy more shares of the stock.

Bonds. If a corporation or government agencies need a loan to expand their organization, they issue bonds in the public market as a way to ask investors to loan money. Bonds are a form of debt and considered a loan made to an issuing corporation or government entity.

Here's another way to explain it. By purchasing bonds, you'll become a creditor (bondholder) loaning money to a corporation or government agency. Think of a bond as an IOU. The entity issuing bonds must pay the bondholder interest on the investment principal based on a promised interest rate for a specified period of time. The interest rate is referred to as the coupon, the final date on which the issuer has to pay interest on the amount borrowed is called the maturity date. When the bond matures, the issuer returns your original investment principal to you.

Mutual funds. A mutual fund is an investment vehicle that holds a pool of dollars in a fund in which investors mutually invest money. The pool of money is managed by a money manager hired by the mutual fund company. A money managers' role is to use the investor's money to buy and sell various types of investment vehicles based on a predetermined investment strategy. These investment vehicles, also known as the mutual fund holdings, collectively make up a portfolio of investments. The portfolio is marketed and sold to investors as shares of the mutual fund. Therefore, each investor becomes a shareholder of the mutual fund represented by a proportionate ownership in each of the mutual fund holdings.

There are many types of mutual funds, and the amount of risk varies widely. As the market conditions change, the share value of a mutual fund will fluctuate up or down and may make or lose money.

Before you invest, a mutual fund company or financial professional recommending the investment is required to provide you with an investment prospectus. A prospectus is an official document that you may get from your investment professional that illustrates details about the mutual fund's risk, investment strategy, fees, and an outlined report of the fund's operations. *You should carefully read the prospectus as well as carefully consider investment objectives, risks, charges, and expenses before investing. Investment return and principal value will fluctuate with changes in market conditions such that shares may be worth more or less than original cost when redeemed, and past mutual fund performance is not a guarantee of future results.*

Types of Investment Accounts

To purchase an investment vehicle, you will need to open an investment account. An investment account, also known as a brokerage account, is the home where your investment vehicles are parked. There are many types of investment accounts in the marketplace. Each serves a specific wealth accumulation purpose.

Investment accounts commonly considered by investors are:

- Non-retirement investment accounts
- 529 Education savings plans
- 401k's and 403b employer sponsored retirement plans
- Individual IRA's and Roth IRA retirement savings accounts

Non-retirement investment accounts are self directed accounts that allow an individual to open an account on their own at a financial institution funded by investment vehicles of their choice. These accounts can be opened individually, joint with other persons, or as a corporation.

529 education savings plans are self directed accounts, established by states or eligible educational institutions, specifically for the purpose of saving for a child's future college costs. An account holder's college education savings investment grows federally tax free as long as withdrawals from the account are for eligible college expenses such as tuition, room, and board. Otherwise, taxes are due on funds not used for these purposes in addition to a 10% IRS federal tax penalty, as well as potential state tax penalties.

401k and **403b** plans are retirement investment accounts set up by employers as a benefit to encourage employees to plan, invest, and build financial security for retirement. These plans have contribution limits that change and increase annually. In 2009, employees may voluntarily contribute up to $16,500 ($22,000 if over 50 years of age) to a 401k or 403b. Contributions are made by having a percentage of income deducted from your paycheck each pay period before income taxes are taken out. Deferring income taxes on payroll contributions made to the account is a tax favored benefit. Income taxes on the contribution and growth of the investments in the retirement account are not payable until a withdrawal is made from the account, typically in retirement. However, taxes are due on any withdrawals, and if made before retirement age 59-1/2, an additional 10% early withdrawal IRS federal tax penalty may apply. An exception to the penalty would include needing money for certain financial hardships. Examples of financial hardship:

- Becoming permanently disabled.
- Payment for a down payment on a primary residence.
- Payment for college education expenses.
- Facing an eviction or foreclosure.

Some 401k and 403b plans may have a loan feature that allows you to borrow funds from your account for any reason as an alternative to taking a withdrawal. In this case, you will borrow money from your retirement savings account and set up an agreement to repay "yourself." This repayment would include the amount borrowed as well as any loan interest changed by the plan.

Under the terms of this agreement income taxes or the 10% penalty are not due on monies repaid to the account.

Traditional IRA's and **Roth IRA's** are two different types of self directed retirement investment accounts each having unique tax favored incentives.

Traditional IRA's:

- Contributions are made with after tax dollars.
- 2009 annual contribution limit is up to $5,000 ($6,000 if over 50 years of age). Limits increase annually thereafter.
- Contributions may be income tax deductible in the year made. Tax deductibility depends on your income and whether you are voluntarily contributing to a retirement account at work.
- Account earnings grow tax deferred until withdrawals are made. Ordinary income taxes are due on withdrawals of previously untaxed amounts (earnings and deductible contributions). Premature withdrawals before age 59-1/2 may be subject to a 10% IRS federal tax penalty.
- You may choose to invest in investment vehicles on any stock exchange including individual stocks, mutual funds, bonds, etc.

Roth IRA's:

- Contributions are made with after tax dollars.
- 2009 annual contribution limit is up to $5,000 ($6,000 if over 50 years of age). Limits increase each year thereafter.
- Contributions are not tax deductible.

- Account earnings grow tax free if held in the account the later of 5 years or until age 59-1/2.
- Premature withdrawals before age 59-1/2 forfeit tax free benefits and are subject to the payment of ordinary income tax on any withdrawn earnings and an additional 10% IRS federal tax penalty.
- You may choose to invest in investment vehicles on any stock exchange including individual stocks, mutual funds, bonds, etc.

Choose and Partner with a Financial Advisor

A financial advisor can help you shape your financial future. A financial advisor can help you formulate an investment strategy considering appropriate investment accounts and vehicles to accomplish your financial goals. Your financial advisor will inform you of the risk vs. reward of a particular investment and help you evaluate your personal tolerance for risk before you invest.

Partner with a financial advisor you can trust and who makes you feel comfortable talking openly about your personal financial information and goals. The best ways to meet a financial advisor is by seeking a referral from a friend, family member, accountant, attorney, or attend investment seminars.

When you have your initial meeting with a financial advisor, treat the meeting as a mutual interview. You want to determine whether the advisor's qualifications, personality and approach are a match for you.

Chapter 3: Financial Wealth Check

Here are five questions you may want to ask:

1. **How long have you been a Financial Advisor?**

   Ask the financial advisor to briefly describe their educational background, work experience, credentials, and if they have any other certifications.

2. **Tell me more about the company you represent?**

   Partner with an advisor working with a company that has a solid reputation in the marketplace and sound financial standing. To review a company's financial stability conduct your due diligence. You can find valuable information on a company's financial viability at www.ambest.com.

3. **What services do you offer?**

   In the market place, there are financial professionals who may only offer insurance plans or just investments. Consider working with a financial professional who represents a company that focuses on helping people design a holistic approach to achieve goals and financial freedom. A holistic approach includes comprehensive financial planning services, investments, and insurance plans.

4. **What is your approach to financial coaching?**

   The financial advisor should have interest in your goals and improving your current financial situation. Ask how often the advisor will meet with you to review your planned investment strategy. You want to work with a financial advisor who spends time educating clients and is interested in having an ongoing one-one relationship with you.

5. **How will I pay for services?**

   A financial advisor is compensated in several ways:

   - Salary paid by the company they represent.
   - Fees that may be hourly, a flat rate, or percentage of your investment.
   - Commissions from financial products that you may implement as a solution for your financial health, goals and wealth building.
   - A combination of fees and commissions.

Building wealth is about developing good habits that must be repeated. But there is one thing that is crucial—understanding that increasing your net worth year after year is simple, but not easy. Living below or within our means is not a difficult concept to understand. Use cash instead of credit cards and spend less money than you make is not rocket science, but for some people it is not easy to do. If you begin living a financial fitness lifestyle and developing good financial habits that must be repeated, you will get closer to your goals and improve your financial well being. Getting control of your money and making good use of it is a battle to be waged every day. It's not easy but I believe that anybody can do it. Stay in tuned with your personal finances and goals.

> **YOUR FINANCIAL FITNESS WORKOUT:**
> **Create A Net Worth Statement**

Getting a grasp on your assets, liabilities and net worth is a basic initial step toward getting you in tuned with your financial direction. Before embarking on increasing your net worth, you need to create a net worth statement and know where you stand financially at this point in time. If this is your first time creating a net worth statement, it is important to know you should not arrive at a "certain number" when you calculate your net worth. Let this be your starting point from where you begin to measure your financial progress.

As you monitor your net worth year to year, your net worth statement will help you chart positive and negative trends in your financial picture and portray whether or not you are getting ahead financially. If you made a blind financial decision and spent your savings, interacting with your net worth statement will shed light on it. If you took on new debt, your net worth statement will remind you. Increased value in your investments or real estate equity will be highlighted on your net worth statement.

Think of your net worth statement as the center piece of your financial picture that you'll reference before any major spending, investing, consideration for credit cards, lines of credit and other financial decisions takes place. These final decisions should be made based on how it will impact your net worth and financial health after careful review of your net worth statement.

There are 3 simple steps to create a net worth statement:
- Choose a system
- List your assets
- List your liabilities

Choose a System

Just like a spending plan, your personality will determine which system is best for you. A pen and paper are just fine. Excel spreadsheets and personal finance software are excellent tools too. At the end of this chapter, you will find a sample net worth statement that you can use as a guide.

List Your Assets and Values

1. Make a list of your assets, everything that you own. The list will include any of the following:
    - Cash: savings, checking, CD's, money market accounts,
    - Investments: stocks, bonds, savings bonds, mutual funds and cash value of life insurance etc.
    - Retirement accounts: include vested company pension, 401k, 403b, Traditional IRA, Roth IRA etc.
    - Real estate, autos, motorcycles, recreational vehicles
    - Collectibles, furniture, jewelry, furs, art, antiques, family heirlooms.
2. Next to each asset, list the current market value, the value you would receive if you sold it today.
3. Total your assets.

List Your Liabilities

1. List your outstanding debts and account balance. This list includes:

    - Real estate mortgage, 2nd mortgage, home equity line of credit, personal loans or lines of credit with the bank, auto loans, etc.
    - Student loans
    - Credit cards
    - Outstanding taxes-local, state, federal, real estate, etc.,
    - Unpaid bills, medical bills, personal loans from family or friends.

2. Total your liabilities.

Calculate And Analyze Your Net Worth

Subtract your total liabilities from your total assets to arrive at your net worth. Is your net worth a positive or a negative number? If you have a positive net worth that is a good sign your wealth building momentum has begun.

Improving a negative net worth is also relative to energizing your wealth building momentum. If you have a negative net worth, do realize a negative net worth can easily be the present reality of someone just starting out on their own or to young families. It may have been necessary for you to finance a college education; therefore you have student loan debt on your net worth statement. It is common for people who are just starting out and young families to have more mortgage debt than equity in their homes. Over time as your real estate appreciates and your mortgage balance decreases your net worth elevates.

Your net worth is a moving target and your goal is to do your best to make it trend upward. Taking steps such as investing as much as you can afford and setting yearly goals to eliminate a portion or all of your debt are likely to increase your net worth overtime. Making it a fun habit to give yourself a financial wealth check up helps you to interact with your financial portrait, update your net worth statement and tally your new standings.

Monitor Your Net Worth

Monitor your net worth statement throughout the year and stay in tuned with your financial picture, especially when making important financial decisions. There may be times when you find yourself recognizing negative as well as positive trends. The road to financial freedom isn't always picturesque and rosy. There will be peaks and valleys as your lifestyle expands and changes course. At times you may feel a financial crunch such as when you are starting a family. Or, the going may get a little tough if you experience a financial setback. Just know that this is par for the course. When the going gets tough, the tough get going. It may be easier said than done. Unfortunately what many people do is bury their heads in the sand and avoid facing the aftermath of financial challenges. If you do this, you may easily lose touch with your financial reality during a time when attention to your personal finances is needed most. The reality is only you can turn your financial challenges into a triumph by taking an active role to seek financial advice on how to make progress by the next year.

Nothing you do is going to change your financial situation overnight but each time you make a sound financial decision it will make a small difference. Every financial decision you make will impact your life over an extended period of time. It is important to keep an open mind about your personal finances, make changes in your course of action when necessary and to stick to your financial goals. Similar to a successful weight loss program, you must change the way you view your financial decisions just as you would view your eating decisions. You must find a plan that works for you, stick to it, and have realistic expectations.

Learn How To Invest

I want you to promise me that you will apply what you learn in this chapter but more importantly take the initiative to increase your level of knowledge in the area of investing. Become proficient and well versed on concepts related to investing and building wealth. At your disposal you have the internet, magazines, books, and personal finance television shows offering financial literacy education. Take advantage of these resources. I would like to issue a challenge to you. Read one book a year on personal finance. There are many perspectives authored by financial professionals, including me. As authors, we publish our point of view with a common goal in mind, to help people change their lives for the better financially. I hope that I am adding value to your lifestyle and you are enjoying my book thus far.

Your 60 Second Cooling Period

As you can see, the key to building wealth is having a disciplined approach to consistently invest and use debt minimally. Stocks, mutual funds, and real estate are the most common investments in the market place used by everyday people to modestly build wealth.

You know debt well. You know where to find it, get it, and use it. You also know debt should be avoided. Debt is a bad influence and will block you from achieving financial freedom. Get to know a financial advisor, mutual funds, and real estate. Know where to find a financial advisor, learn how to invest in mutual funds and purchase real estate.

Make a pledge to get into the wealth zone. Imagine having $10,000 in your savings account, $25,000 in a mutual fund, or $100,000 in your 401k. How would that feel? That is a good start and a good phase one goal for financial freedom. It is not impossible to achieve when you make the decision to increase your net worth every year.

Chapter 4

Debt or Pride?

The Skit

> **Debt:** "You are approved for a $2500 credit card limit. I know you're good for it because you pay other credit cards on time. But, instead of using their money, use mine; I'll do you a favor by charging less interest. If you really do right by me and pay on time, I may give you an increased credit limit next year. Now go on and buy yourself something you can't afford. It is on me."

> **Pride:** "Debt, I fell for your tricks in the past but you will not fool me this time. I don't need your money. You see, I am happy with what I have. I am strong enough to save money on my own for things I want. AND, my savings will earn interest instead of giving interest payments to you in unreasonable amounts. Debt, you got your eyes on my future and so do I. The difference is I see my future without you."

Debt

Debt happens. Debt may happen because of life events that were out of your control like a serious accident or illness keeping you out of work, and losing your job. Unforeseen events like these can end your income and consequently, you may wipe out your savings. Without long term financial security to back you up, you might be lead easily to the debt trap.

Or, you may be contributing willingly to your debt issues by borrowing money from credit cards to buy fine dining, lunch, groceries, take out, entertainment, travel, clothing, appliances, electronics, computer downloads, gas, etc. Then there are mortgages, student loans, and auto loans. And what about monthly service bills for satellite TV, premium cable channels, utilities, cell phone bills, gym memberships, over due bills? Before you know it, your monthly debt obligations are exceeding your take home pay robbing you of peace of mind and a quality life. It does not stop there. Outstanding balances on your bills, loans, and credit cards must be paid in full eventually. Keeping up with your debt load can be challenging. One false move by making late payments will cause your credit score to decline.

There aren't many instances more frustrating than to work very hard for your money and at the end of the work week give a good amount of your take home pay to bills and creditors. Gone are the days when people took pride in not owing anyone debt. Ask your grand parents and great grand parents what having debt means to them. Their generation viewed being in debt to anyone is disgraceful or appalling. Owing anyone or any entity money was seen as a smear on the family name. Family security, pride and preserving the family's modest wealth were highest priority for previous generations. A quality life and financial security are what previous generations worked hard to maintain with pride.

Today's young adult generation works hard to maintain credit card bills that bought everyday expenses, keeping up with the Jones', instant gratification etc. Today's generation willingly promises their future income to finance companies with an interest rate of 10-29%. Could it be that in the 21st century debt is stronger than pride?

Pride

Pride is having a strong sense of self respect and refusing any occasion to be humiliated. Pride also means feeling joyful for your accomplishments. I mentioned family pride, financial security, and preserving the family's modest wealth were highest priority for previous generations. However, these family or personal values are no longer a prominent presence in the lifestyle of many people living during our lifetime. The negative influence of debt has successfully penetrated the lifestyles of young adults who allowed debt to strip away their pride, and financial future.

Here's how:

- "Can I put this on your charge ma'am?"
- "Sir, would you like to save 10% on your purchase by opening up a charge account today?"

- "Receive 20% off your purchase today if you use your department store credit card."
- "No closing cost cash out refinance home loan, call today for a consultation."
- "Take it home today with our 90 day same as cash credit card, if you qualify."

Sounds familiar? We're you ever enticed by credit offers? It happened to me. I found myself taking advantage of offers for credit cards on my college campus. Getting approved for credit was exciting to me. After I opened up credit card accounts on campus, I headed for the mall and opened department store credit cards. I had about 8 open credit card accounts maxed out when I was 24 years old. Frankly, I was operating terribly irresponsible but yet had not realized my poor spending behavior. Having credit cards felt like a privilege to me. Little did I know my values and pride were not well represented and I compromised my financial future. It wasn't until my future paycheck went mostly to my debt load that having credit cards did not feel so good anymore. I felt like the monthly payments would never end. I was trapped in debt and did not know how to set myself free.

Often times people do not realize they have a debt problem until it is too late, piled high and out of control. If this is you, don't be dismayed because there is a way to reclaim your pride and prosperity. Life after debt really does exist! Life after debt begins when you resist the urge to rely on credit cards, get in tuned with your money and nurture a wealth building mindset.

> **CHANGE YOUR LIFE
> FOR THE BETTER FINANCIALLY**
>
> Simple Step #4:
> Nurture a Wealth
> Building Mindset

The Wealth Building Mindset

Combating debt issues begins with making up your mind to experience financial freedom in your lifetime. It doesn't just take money and a debt management plan to slim and trim your debt. It takes a wealth building mindset. Otherwise, if you are not nurturing a wealth building mindset, once you pay off your debt load, you will more than likely run your balances back up again.

A wealth building mindset entails thinking, decision making and spending behavior that support putting your money to work in ways that promotes financial wellness and accumulating wealth. People with a wealthy mindset know that debt cancels wealth, deflates their net worth, and is a barrier to their financial freedom. Therefore, debt is a hindrance to a quality lifestyle and wealth accumulation; credit card financing and excessive loans are not an option for a wealthy mindset thinker.

Wealth building thinkers live below their means and purposefully delay instant gratification for things that they cannot afford. You see the difference between people who are building wealth modestly and people who aren't is not how much discretionary income they have or don't have for savings and investments. It is neither their possessions or about the luxuries their financial wealth can buy that makes the difference. The difference is mindset. People who nurture a wealth building mindset are successfully living a quality lifestyle or have attained financial freedom because they made a conscious decision to live this way.

Nurturing a Wealth Building Mindset

Nurturing a wealth building mindset involves cultivating seeds and deeds of good financial health. You have the choice to plant a seed for anything that you want to grow and care for. The seeds of any garden require time, patience and nurtured soil in order to blossom bountifully and keep weeds at bay. Seeds for growth in values, pride, and wealth similarly need cultivation. For, if you are not nurturing and cultivating a wealth building mindset, debt weeds may grow in your personal finances, affect the quality of your life and stunt your growth.

Have you ever seen a garden or yard heavily infested with weeds? What an eye sore right? Someone let the weeds get out of hand and contaminate the garden. Weeds surface naturally in a garden. Weeds love open space and full access to the sun to thrive. In this space, weeds seize the opportunity to claim a share of the yard. However, weeds are not the cause of an unhealthy garden but rather a garden lacking nurturing gives birth to imbedded weeds.

Having debt is like having weeds in your personal finances. Where there is creditworthiness and wealth, debt weeds begin to surface in the form of credit offers. This is the space where creditors seek to thrive and seize an opportunity to claim an imbedded stake in your green. Nonetheless offers for credit are not the cause of debt weeds in finances. Instead, lack of nurturing a wealth building mindset yields decisions to accept unnecessary credit offers; the outcome can be a debt ridden lifestyle.

If you have debt weeds imbedded in your personal finances, believe that you can do better and quickly address any thriving debt. There is room for improvement in everyone's life. To assist you, I am offering the following three seeds for a wealth building mindset that you can plant and nurture.

1. A decision to achieve financial freedom in your lifetime
2. Sensible gratification
3. A debt elimination plan

A Decision, Financial Freedom

Deciding to achieve financial freedom in your lifetime is the seed that you plant in your mind to grow wealth. Envision waking up each day having no worries about debt or your credit score's buying power, plenty of money in the bank for unexpected opportunities or emergencies. Imagine living your life with no financial barriers, making a difference in your community, and most of all fulfilling the goals and dreams that live within your heart. We live with the results of our decisions good or bad. If this is so, why not decide to be financially free?

Once you decide to achieve financial freedom in your lifetime, your next bold step is to back up your decision with conviction and a strong wealth ethic. Ethics represent a system of moral standards and principles. In order to develop a strong wealth ethic, you will need to recognize and adopt moral standards and principles that support your financial well being and desire to build wealth. The following ten building blocks of wealth ethics serve as a guide to a moral and principled approach to create wealth.

Ten Building Blocks of Wealth Ethics

1. **Educate yourself on financial matters and wealth creation.** Attend financial empowerment seminars and workshops. Read financial books and magazines to increase your knowledge of personal money management and wealth accumulation. Learn more about the resources that you will need to accomplish your goals and apply what you learn.

2. **Have faith in yourself and stay motivated.** Know that you are capable of achieving financial freedom. You may not have ever done it yet. But know that "you can" do it. If you have faith in yourself and "decide" that you can achieve anything that you desire, you will give birth to goals, plans to achieve your goals, fortitude to withstand any personal or financial challenge, and passion to put your best foot forward to be successful.

3. **Be goal oriented.** Put your goals in writing and create a plan to achieve them. Where is your life heading? Personally? Professionally? Financially? It is easier to achieve your goals if you make them more real by putting your goals in writing. Then frequently review your goals and your planned strategy toward accomplishment. Always be aware of where you are in the plan. If you fall off track, pick back up where you left off.

4. **Live within your means.** Live within your financial reality. Know how much money is coming into your household and how much money it takes to finance your lifestyle and goals.

Make the most of your financial resources by following a spending plan every month that includes a financial strategy to pay yourself first.

5. **Pay yourself first.** Modestly build wealth by paying yourself first on a consistent basis. Consider investing a set dollar amount each month toward long term financial security. It is not so much the dollar amount you pay yourself first and invest along the way, but the consistency with time. There are various types of financial vehicles that can help you build wealth. A financial advisor can help you make informed choices about saving and investing in your financial future.

6. **Use cash instead of credit cards.** Choose pride over debt. Pay cash for things rather than using your credit card. If you use your credit card for purchases, only do so with the intent to pay off the balance at the end of the month.

7. **Create an insurance portfolio. Insurance plans protect you from unexpected events that may create a financial need.**

    For example:
    - Death of someone you depend on financially.
    - A temporary or permanent sickness that prevents you from being able to work and earn an income.
    - An unfortunate accident or natural disaster that damages your property or inflicts serious costly personal injuries.

    Adequate insurance coverage may prevent you from going into debt or spending down your accumulated wealth to weather a financial storm that any of the above situations may cause. Review chapter six for details on this topic.

8. **Elevate your Net Worth Year after Year.** Make it your goal to increase your net worth annually. This can be done by simply adding to the value of your assets while at the same time decreasing your liabilities. Let your net worth statement and annual financial check up serve as your wealth building report card.

9. **Take responsibility for your actions and circumstances.** Intentionally create winning circumstances by choosing thoughts, actions and spending behavior that positively support your goals and financial well being. Think with the end in mind. What is the outcome that you would like to live with? When you choose thoughts, actions or behavior you are choosing the outcome.

10. **Partner with a Financial Coach.** A financial coach, otherwise known as a financial advisor, can help you shape your financial future.

Sensible Gratification

The seed of sensible gratification curbs impulse shopping and sprouts guidance on how to spend your money in ways that make sense for you both financially and emotionally. We live in a world that promotes consumerism and instant gratification despite the fact that it is detrimental to your financial health. People want the coolest tech gadgets, the latest fashions, the best dining restaurant, exotic vacations, and the best of the best right now this very second. Consequently, cravings for instant gratification are impulsively resolved by many people using "easy credit" and lots of discretionary

Chapter 4: Debt or Pride?

spending. Rarely do people stop and think about the emotional price to pay for accumulating debt and spending extra money that can go toward building wealth.

When I was a young adult, I became accustomed to using credit cards and paying unreasonable interest for "things" I wanted "now" which was immediately consumed or ignored in the next day, month or year. Yet when the vacation ended, the clothes are worn out, or "things" go out of style, I would still have the credit card bills for those items and not feeling very good about it. Undoubtedly, the outcome was cancelled wealth and exorbitant compounding interest applied to my credit card balance. Without a doubt using credit cards is not a sensible, viable decision financially. What about emotional sensibility? How can an outcome like this affect you emotionally?

Emotionally, credit card debt and excessive loans are the most taxing ways to finance your lifestyle. Debt feels like a heavy burden that brings up feelings of regret, shame, or animosity. Negative feelings come with the territory of debt and pours over into other areas of your lifestyle affecting you emotionally, your health, relationships, and how you continue to manage your financial affairs. Some people find themselves so deep in the debt trap that they bury their heads in the sand and do nothing to dig out. Their financial lives remain stagnant because they chose to allow debt weeds to grow and remain. Meanwhile, if only instant gratification was delayed or excessive spending was contained, they just might be building wealth for financial freedom.

Delaying gratification does not mean that you cannot spend money on things that you want. Sensibly delaying gratification serves a greater purpose. It means making conscious choices to spend money in ways that does not jeopardize your financial health, emotional well being, achieving your goals or building wealth. It means demonstrating behavior that supports an outcome that you can happily live with emotionally as well as financially.

Debt Elimination Plan

Implementing a debt elimination plan is like planting a seed for a breath of fresh air. It is a seed you can nurture for a fresh start to grow healthier and stronger emotionally and financially. A wonderful life after debt exists! If you have debt, for your benefit, put a debt elimination plan in place that has a palatable approach that you can nurture within a reasonable amount of time.

Are you willing to nurture a second job for six months to a year so that you can bring home extra income that can be used to knock out your debt? Are you willing to shave expenses in your spending plan? Shop less? Dine out less, etc? How committed will you become to nurture a wealth building mindset?

Eliminating and avoiding debt is ingrained in the mind of a wealth building thinker. As you eliminate debt, your net worth increases. When you eliminate debt wouldn't you rather invest your former monthly debt payments in a long term investment such as real estate, stocks, or mutual funds to create wealth? Of course you would. After all haven't you already made the decision to achieve financial freedom in your lifetime and make decisions that support your desired outcome? I hope so.

Chapter 4: Debt or Pride?

There is a quality life without debt waiting for you. You may be thinking now is a good time to address your debt load and put a plan into play to get rid of it. Here are the signs:

- You maxed out your credit cards.
- Your credit card balances exceed $2500.
- You can only afford the minimum monthly payment.
- You skip payments on some bills in order to pay other creditors.
- You were turned down for credit.
- You are not sure about what is reported on your credit reports.
- You use credit cards to buy everyday basic needs.
- You avoid the mail box or ignore credit card statements.
- You don't have an emergency fund.
- You don't have a plan to pay off your credit card debt.

For every potential warning sign above, there is a solution. If you identify with the warning signs there is only one thing you must do right away, seek the help of a professional consumer credit counselor who can partner with you to create a plan to get rid of your debt.

Consumer Credit Counseling Services (CCCS) is a non-profit consumer service agency that provides confidential financial counseling, community wide education programs in money management, debt management programs for consumers who are over extended and comprehensive home buying counseling. There are agencies strategically located across the country in a city near you.

CCCS partners with you to help alleviate your debt issues by helping you put a debt repayment plan in place. A debt repayment plan maps out the steps to erase your credit card debt within a specified time frame. By partnering with a professional consumer credit counselor, you will earn an advocate coaching you to a zero balance on your credit cards.

Your consumer credit counselor will step in and be the middle person between you and your creditors renegotiating lowering your interest rates, payment terms and remove excessive fees charged by lenders. Your debt repayment plan will be customized to help you regain control of your cash flow and wisely manage your debt in an affordable way. Plus, your plan will define the amount of time required before you become debt free. Once you've completed your debt management plan, CCCS has programs that will teach you how to reestablish your credit and improve your credit score.

Promise yourself that you will seek professional guidance to put a plan into play to cut the weeds! Shame and the feeling of embarrassment hold people back from getting the help that they need to get out of debt. Actually, the true perception is the opposite. You will be commended when you reach for the light at the end of the tunnel and make an effort to create wealth. Partnering with a consumer credit counselor demonstrates that you are taking pride in making your financial health better, increasing your net worth by decreasing your debt, and eventually regaining full control of future income that you can direct toward building freedom.

CCCS offers 3 ways to engage in consumer credit counseling services: in person, by telephone, or online!

Consumer Credit Counseling Services

1-800-251-CCCS (24/7)

www.cccsinc.org

Schedule an appointment with yourself to contact CCCS or visit the website to arrange your initial counseling session. Either way, I encourage you to visit the website and learn more about the services of CCCS. Take advantage of the online tools and resources that are available to you at no charge. On the website, you will be able to chat with a counselor, take a self evaluation of your present credit issues, and receive immediate feedback and direction on the next steps to take to improve your situation.

> **YOUR FINANCIAL FITNESS WORKOUT:**
> **Nurture A Wealth Building Mindset**

Nurture a wealth building mindset and clear any debt weeds once and for all. Empower yourself to plant and nurture the three seeds of a wealth building mindset:

#1 **Your Decision to Achieve Financial Freedom In Your Lifetime**
Take the **Ten Building Blocks of Wealth Ethics** everywhere you go.
1. Educate Yourself on Financial Matters
2. Have Faith in Yourself and Stay Motivated To Achieve Financial Freedom

3. Be Goal Oriented
4. Live Within Your Means
5. Pay Yourself First
6. Use Cash Instead of Credit Cards
7. Create an Insurance Portfolio
8. Elevate Your Net Worth Year After Year
9. Take Responsibility for Your Actions and Circumstances
10. Partner With A Financial Coach.

Additional nurturing: Read one personal finance book a year and subscribe to a personal finance magazine via online or retail.

#2 Sensible Gratification

Just because we live in a world that promotes consumerism doesn't mean you have to participate to your detriment. You have a greater purpose for your time, energy and hard earned dollars. Sensibly make these resources work for you. Be mindful of the emotional as well as the financial sensibility of your thoughts, actions, and decisions. The choice is always yours to decide on what type of outcome you wish to create. Weeds grow in personal finances when nurturing a wealth building mindset is ignored. What's the choice you will make?

Additional nurturing: Place your written goals in a place where you can see them everyday. Visualize achieving your goals daily. Visualize achieving financial freedom once a day. Believe in yourself.

#3 A Debt Elimination Plan

Partner with a consumer credit counselor to map out a plan to eliminate your debt.

- Visit www.cccsinc.org to learn more about Consumer Credit Counseling Services.
- Set an appointment for a counseling session within the next 10 business days.
- Prepare for your session. What to ask:
  1. What is the cost? In most cases, credit counseling is free. Starting a debt management plan may cost an average $35 per month.
  2. If you choose an agency in your local area, ask if the agency is certified and accredited. Certified counselors pass rigorous tests so that they can offer experience and expert knowledge.
  3. Is the approach comprehensive? Ideally you want to work with an agency that offers more than debt elimination planning. Consider working with an agency that offers an empowering holistic approach incorporating spending plan counseling and educational programs that enhance financial fitness.

Additional nurturing: Work diligently to transform your monthly debt payments into wealth creation.

Your 60 Second Cooling Period

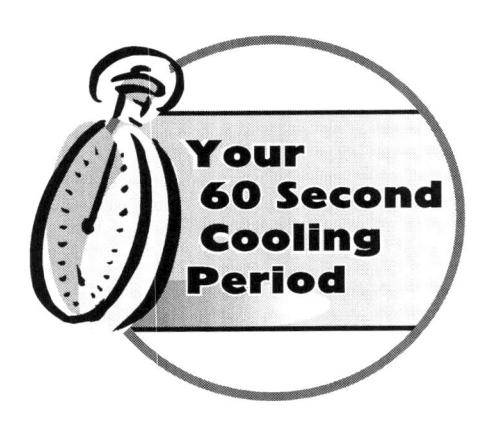

Be Wealthy.

CHAPTER 5

THE PULSE OF YOUR CREDIT SCORE

Sometimes you just don't realize the importance and value of having good credit until you need it and don't have it. Have you checked the pulse of your credit score lately? It is not just that you will need good credit to get an auto loan or mortgage. Your credit history determines what interest rate you will pay. Auto insurance companies and apartment communities use your credit report during their decision making process. Employers conduct credit checks as part of the hiring process. Do you have a dream of starting your own business? Are you planning to apply for a small business loan? What will your credit report reveal when a financial institution requests a copy to determine your credit worthiness? Utility services, cable TV, telephone, and cellular phone companies want to know your credit history too. If it is not up to par, these consumer service companies will demand a security deposit or worst case scenario you may get declined.

Establishing a good credit history has never been as significant as it is today. That is why it is so important to be sensible and responsible when using debt. Your credit score and credit report are considered your financial resume. It speaks volumes on your behalf.

With so much at stake, I encourage you to become well versed on how your credit score is calculated. If you don't know your credit score, check what is being reported in your credit files soon.

> **CHANGE YOUR LIFE FOR THE BETTER FINANCIALLY**
>
> **Simple Step #5:
> Check The Pulse of Your
> Credit Score Annually**

What is a Credit Score?

Credit scoring is a numeric formula developed by Fair Isaac and Company (FICO) that compiles information about past and present credit history found in your credit reports as reported by the three major credit bureaus: Equifax, Experian, and Trans Union. FICO gathers data about positive and negative payment history, how much you owe, and types of credit lines found on each credit report. Once the data is compiled, FICO uses a formula to rate your creditworthiness using a 3-digit number ranging from 300-934. This is your credit score.

A credit score of 700 or above is an excellent credit score and lets decision makers know you are in good financial health with low credit risk of paying on time or in full. On the other hand, credit scores below 600 serves as a red flag to lenders and companies of interest announcing you are a high credit risk. Your score may be below 600 if your total debt load is above average, you are not paying bills on time or you have liens and judgments for unpaid bills recorded on your credit report.

If your credit score is teetering within 600-700, decision makers may scrutinize your credit reports to ascertain whether you are heading in the direction of good financial health or on the verge of a financial downfall.

Five Parts of Your FICO Score

FICO's computation method analyzes five parts of your credit report. These important details will represent the pulse of your credit score.

- **Payment History:** accounts for 35% of your FICO score. What they are looking at in this category is your track record. Are you paying your creditors on time? How many accounts show no late payments? Do you have any late payments, bankruptcy, judgments or other negative items? How late are your payments? How much is owed on delinquent accounts and how recent the occurrence? How many delinquencies are there?

    Tips:
    - Paying on time attributes a strong credit score.
    - If you missed some payments, bring your account current and begin to pay bills on time. Showing some positive history following a delinquency can help your score over the long term.
    - If you are having trouble making payments, seek the assistance of a Certified Consumer Credit Counselor who can partner with you to put a debt management

plan in place and help you get on track to making timely payments.

- **How Much You Owe:** accounts for 30% of your FICO score. This category considers how much of your available credit limit is used. Maxing out credit cards and loans lowers your credit score. Believe it or not, if more than 30% of your available credit is used, it is viewed as you are overextended and in some kind of financial trouble.

  Tips:
  - Keep your lines of credit balances at or below 30% of available credit.
  - If your balances are above 30%, work at paying the balance down so that you can increase your credit score.

- **Length of Credit History:** accounts for 15% of your FICO score. This category considers how established your credit history is. The longer your credit history the more beneficial for your FICO score. A longer credit history will increase your score. This does not mean having new or short credit history will not get you a high score. If your credit history is new or short, your credit score will be based on your payment history, available credit, and types of credit lines.

  Tips:
  - Refrain from opening many new accounts frivolously. Opening new accounts actually lower your average account age and affect your credit score negatively. This holds true even if you have a long credit history.

- **New Credit:** accounts for 10% of your FICO score. The new credit category evaluates the number of credit inquiries and new lines of credit are listed on your credit report. When you allow your credit to be pulled multiple times or you have opened multiple accounts in a short length of time, your score may decrease. Multiple inquiries and opening multiple new accounts also signals you may be on the verge of overextending yourself. FICO will be looking at:

- How many new accounts are on your credit report and how long it has been since you applied for credit or opened new accounts?
- How many credit inquiries are on your credit report?
- Do you have a good recent history following past payment delinquencies?

Tips:
- When seeking a mortgage or auto loan and shopping for best interest rates, rate shop within a short period of time, usually 30 days. Doing so may not affect your credit score and the perception will be you are shopping for the best loan.
- Forego the temptation to open new accounts to buy things you cannot afford to pay with cash.
- If you have late payment history or credit problems in the past, open a new account with the intent to be responsible and rebuild your credit history. Paying on time will increase your score and re-establish your credit.
- **Types of Credit You Are Using:** about 10% of your FICO score. With the types of credit category FICO analyzes your mix of credit cards, retail accounts, personal loans, auto, and mortgage etc.. It is not necessary to have one of each line of

credit. Usually people with longer credit history tend to have a mix and it can add to their scores.

Tips:

- Do not open accounts seeking to create a better credit mix. It may decrease your score. Only apply for credit as needed....ideally to finance an asset.

Special Note: Because your FICO report is derived from information recorded in your credit report whether accurate or inaccurate, it is very important to check your credit report annually to be sure it does not contain any discrepancies.

How To Check Your Credit Score

You have three FICO scores to keep track of; one at each of the three credit reporting bureaus. Each year check the pulse of your credit score at each credit bureau. Although it is the goal for FICO to keep the scores at each credit bureau consistent, you may find that your score at each agency varies by a few points. This variation may differ because:

- There may be varied information reported on your credit report at each agency.
- The credit reporting bureaus may record and publish information given by creditors in different ways.

You can learn more information about credit scoring and purchase all three FICO scores online or by telephone at:

www.myfico.com

1-800-342-6742

Checking Your Credit Report

It is recommended to check your credit report annually or at least six months before you are planning to have your credit report and credit score pulled by a lender or employer. Residents in every state have the right to obtain one free credit report per year from each credit bureau. Your complimentary credit report is offered through Annual Credit Report Request Service. To receive your free annual credit report submit a request by mail, phone, or online:

Annual Credit Report Request Service
P.O. Box 105281
Atlanta, GA 30348-5281
1-877-FACT-ACT
www.annualcreditreport.com

Additional copies of your credit report can be purchased directly from each of the major credit reporting agencies.

Equifax	**Experian**	**TransUnion**
www.equifax.com	www.experian.com	www.transunion.com
1-800-685-1111	1-800-200-6020	1-800-888-4213

Comb Your Report For Errors

Once you receive your credit reports, use a highlighter pen and comb each report for errors. You want to make sure the information in your credit file is accurate so that your financial resume will garner fair, favorable consideration. Review the following for accuracy:

- Your name, address, telephone number, current employer etc.

- Accurate status of your accounts, payment history, credit limit, available credit etc
- Status of any delinquent accounts, liens, judgments, collection accounts, bankruptcy
- Accounts that you did not open; fraud
- Types of accounts open
- Types of accounts closed
- Any unusual discrepancy

If you notice fraudulent activity on your credit report, contact the credit reporting agency immediately. Give the agency an explanation of the fraudulent account and ask that a fraud alert be placed on your credit file. Then contact your creditors and do the same. Also contact your local police department and file a police report.

Dispute Errors On Your Credit Report

Act right away to dispute and correct derogatory errors on your credit reports. Each credit reporting agency has a dispute process. The dispute process is a formal investigative step consumers may utilize to inform the credit bureau of errors on their credit report. Equifax, Experian, and Trans Union make it easy and simple to submit a dispute. Here's the way it works:

- You can begin an investigation by writing a letter to the credit bureau via mail or submit a dispute via the credit bureau's website. The most efficient way to initiate a dispute is on the credit bureau's website. The step by step online dispute process is user friendly.

Chapter 5: The Pulse of Your Credit Score

- Once the credit bureau receives your request, they will contact the source to be investigated on your behalf free of charge. They will request proof of valid account details from the source. If you have supporting documentation that proves the account status is invalid, you may submit the documentation to the credit bureau when you initiate the investigation.
- If the source investigated provides valid proof that justifies the disputed error, the credit bureau will inform you of the results and the account status will remain unchanged on your credit report.
- If the source does not provide valid proof or does not respond to the credit bureau's dispute within 30 days, the credit bureau will delete the disputed account from your file and mail an updated credit report to you.

Derogatory information on your credit report whether accurate or inaccurate can hurt your credit score and remain on your credit report for 2-10 years depending on what type of information is being reported. Once the delinquent reporting time has expired, the credit reporting agency will delete the negative history from your file and as a result your credit score will improve.

Stay in tuned with the number of years until the delinquency falls off your credit report. Take note:

- **Late payments:** a 30-180 day delinquency may stay on your report for 7 years.
- **Collection accounts:** remains on your report for 7 years. The clock starts ticking 181 days from the most recent delinquent

period that precedes the account getting set up at the collection agency. If you paid this account in full, the account should be marked "paid collection" on your credit report.

- **Judgements, charged- off accounts, and tax liens:** will remain for 7 years.
- **Bankruptcy:** typically remains for 10 years
- **Inquiries:** When a creditor checks your credit report, it is called a hard inquiry. When an employer, utility or insurance company checks your credit it is called a soft inquiry. Hard inquiries may remain on your report for 2 years. Soft inquiries do not affect your credit score.
- **Closed Accounts:** If you closed an account that has a delinquency reported, it will remain on your credit report for 7 years.

Your Financial Fitness Workout:
Check The Pulse Of Your Credit Score Annually

Step One: Check The Pulse of Your Credit Scores

Each year check your Equifax, Experian, and Trans Union credit score. Contact:

www.myfico.com

1-800-342-6742

Step Two: Order Credit Reports

Take advantage of your free annual credit report. Contact:

Annual Credit Report Request Service
P.O. Box 105281
Atlanta, GA 30348-5281
1-877-FACT-ACT
www.annualcreditreport.com

Step Three: Comb Your Credit Report for Errors

Review your report for accuracy including your personal information such as name, address, date of birth, telephone number, employer information etc. Highlight any error found on your credit report.

Step Four: Dispute Errors

Get familiar with the dispute process by visiting the credit reporting agency's website and prepare yourself for submitting a dispute. Although you can request a dispute by mail or telephone, the online method is simple and easiest. If you use the online method, the agency will send you an email to let you know the results can be viewed online. You'll also receive a hard copy of your updated credit report in the mail.

Step Five: Clean Up Your Credit Report

Work at improving your creditworthiness. Set a goal each year to improve your credit score. Examples of ways to improve your credit score:

- Pay on time; pay your account in full.
- Pay down debt below 30% of the available credit.

- Dispute errors
- Make payments on time following a delinquency
- Partner with a Consumer Credit Counselor to help you get your credit in order.

Your 60 Second Cooling Period

Sometimes you just don't realize the importance and value of something until it is gone. Do your best to protect, preserve, and value what matters most in your world.

CHAPTER 6

WEIGH IN: PROTECT WHAT YOU VALUE

Let's take a moment to go back to the first chapter of this book. What led you here? Weigh in again on what you value and why you decided on taking steps to change your life for the better financially. Would you do anything in your power to protect anyone or anything that you value from harm? You would protect your family. Right? What about your lifestyle? Would you protect your lifestyle from financial harm? How? For starters, using credit cards excessively may harm your financial health for many years ahead. So you may want to start there? You can also protect yourself from financial harm by having an emergency fund. Can you think of any other occurrences that may financially harm your lifestyle? Here are a couple of examples:

- If you were out of work recovering from an illness or accident for 7 months, how would you pay your basic living expenses without a regular pay check coming in?
- If you died tomorrow, would your spouse/partner or children's emotional pain be compounded by financial suffering because you did not have any or enough life insurance?

Expected or unexpected catastrophic events like these can place our lifestyle in financial harms way. We face a myriad of risks beyond our control that can negatively impact our lifestyle financially. Such is a part of life. Life's inherent financial risk can potentially obstruct our financial success and cause financial suffering. So, we must put an insurance portfolio of various types of insurance plans in place to protect our valued lifestyle from life's unpredictable financial storms.

Common financial storms that can harm you financially are:

1. Loss of financial support due to death of a loved one.
2. Not having a regular paycheck because an accident or illness keeps you out of work for an extended period of time or permanently.
3. Medical bills adding up for healthcare treatments and surgical procedures.
4. Getting sued for claims and damages from automobile or other unfortunate accidents caused by you.
5. Having damage or destruction of your home after a natural disaster.

Insurance plans can protect you from all of those cases of potential financial harm if you have a sufficient amount of insurance coverage. Otherwise without insurance protection or enough coverage, you will pay money out of your pocket to replace the value of what you lost. You cannot prevent unexpected catastrophic events from happening to you. But you can protect yourself and your family from suffering financially as a result of the outcome. Take the appropriate measures to shield yourself from a financial storm by assembling an insurance portfolio of various types of insurance plans with adequate coverage, which is the 6th simple step to change your life for the better financially.

> **CHANGE YOUR LIFE FOR THE BETTER FINANCIALLY**
>
> **Simple Step #6:
> Assemble An Insurance Portfolio
> With Adequate Protection**

An insurance portfolio contains a diverse line up of insurance plans offering financial protection in multiple areas of your lifestyle. At the very least, your insurance portfolio should have six types of insurance coverage:

1. Automobile
2. Homeowner's/Renter's
3. Liability
4. Health
5. Disability
6. Life

Most people have a love-hate relationship with insurance. They hate paying the premiums, but love it when they're in a car accident and collect a settlement check for pain and financial suffering from an insurance company. What if it was the other way around? What if someone wanted to sue you because you caused an auto accident? Are you prepared for the worst outcome financially? With too little insurance coverage, beyond experiencing physical or emotional trauma, you are bound to suffer financially as well.

So what is the best way to determine the proper amount of insurance coverage to have? Simply by consulting with an insurance professional and assess the 'value' of what you are protecting. Why should you have an insurance portfolio? To protect the financial well being of you and your loved ones, your lifestyle's goals, and your wealth.

I am going to walk you through the points to consider when evaluating your needs for insurance while assembling an insurance portfolio. Then with confidence, you can arrange to meet with an insurance professional who can help you implement insurance policies that are suitable for your lifestyle. Naturally, you would like to pay affordable insurance premiums for each type of insurance plan. Ideally, you want to consider adequate insurance protection. Step up and properly protect what you value.

Weigh In: Auto Insurance

Your Auto. Repairing and replacing your vehicle is not your primary concern when evaluating your needs for auto insurance coverage. Car insurance companies will only pay claims for a totaled vehicle based on the book value of your car. The monies paid to you by the insurance company may not even be enough to buy a new car, especially if you have an auto loan to pay off or if you do not have gap insurance. In these instances, most people need to tap their savings to come up with a down payment for a car when their car is totaled. Here's where your emergency fund can rescue you. If auto insurance is not designed to replace a totaled car with a new vehicle, what is auto insurance really for? To protect you from claims and lawsuits that may stack up against you because the "accident" was your fault.

We live in a society that favors lawsuits based on negligence. In today's time, insurance settlements are awarded larger dollar amounts more than ever. One serious auto accident can bankrupt a person if they are not well protected financially by auto insurance or additional personal liability insurance. Auto insurance can offer financial relief so that you may not need to liquidate your savings, mutual funds, stocks, real estate etc., to satisfy claims against you. Auto insurance is designed to protect the wealth you've worked so hard to accumulate.

25/50/25? 50/100/50? 100/300/100?

According to state law, you are required to carry three types of liability coverage on your auto policy:

- Bodily Injury Liability
- Property Liability
- Uninsured/Underinsured Liability (some states may not require)

Liability as it relates to your insurance protection is a legally imposed obligation under the law based on damages caused by you. Auto liability insurance pays for claims if the accident is your fault. Auto liability coverage is described by using three numbers like 100/300/100. These numbers are called the split limits of liability insurance. Your state of residence will mandate a required minimum for split limits of liability coverage that all registered vehicles must have. The state law wants to be sure you have a minimum level of liability insurance just in case you accidentally harm someone or destroy property using your vehicle.

For example, the state of Georgia's minimum is 25/50/25. This translates as:

- $25k of bodily injury coverage caused to another person/
- $50k of coverage for total bodily injuries caused to everyone in accident/
- $25k of coverage for property damage

Auto insurance companies offer coverage that exceeds the state's minimum so that you can add extra financial protection for your personal interests. The split limits of liability coverage that you choose are the maximum dollars the insurance company will pay on your behalf per accident. If you are at fault in a major auto collision and damages exceed the coverage limits in your auto policy, you are on the hook to pay the difference.

Evaluating Your Personal Interests

It is common for people to be motivated by lenders to buy car and home insurance to protect their ability to pay off the loan in the event the car or home becomes completely destroyed. In this case, you are protecting your lender's interest by "supposedly" buying enough insurance to payoff the loan if necessary. Think about this, what about you? Have you considered your personal interests?

State minimum requirements for auto coverage may be enough for a minor fender bender or a collision with one car. Keep in mind, the minimum protection may not satisfy the liability associated with a major auto accident. Major collisions can cause serious bodily injuries and multiple casualties. Do you have enough wealth to pay out of pocket for a major liability if you are underinsured? Better yet, are you comfortable risking the wealth you've accumulated to pay for claims because you caused an accident? Your future earnings and income can be up for grabs too if you are not well protected.

Before choosing split limits of liability or any other features of an auto insurance policy, evaluate your personal interests. There are three points to consider:

1. Total Value of Your Assets
2. Your Risk Tolerance
3. Worst Case Scenario

Total Value of Your Assets

What is the total value of your assets? I am not referring to your net worth. Instead consider the total value of the assets listed on your net worth statement. These assets are at risk if claims are brought against you if you are underinsured. Take into consideration split limits of liability that protect the *value* of your assets.

> For example: Let's say you live in Georgia and your assets total $120,000 and your existing auto policy's split limits are 25/50/25. Let's also factor, you do not have a separate personal liability insurance policy. In this scenario, you have not fully protected the value of your wealth. Your wealth's exposure to financial risk is $95k-$70k-$95k ($120,000 – the split limits.) If you were in a car accident and damages exceeded 25/50/25 you will be forced to tap your assets to pay the difference. How would that make you feel? Would you be comfortable risking a loss of 120,000 or more?

Risk Tolerance

After asking yourself whether or not you have enough coverage to protect your assets, through the example, you may already be getting a sense of your risk tolerance. Similar to when investing money in the stock market, risk tolerance equates to your comfort zone with any exposure to risk. Let's call it the sleep factor for concept purposes.

If the total value of your assets is $120,000, can you sleep at night knowing each time you drive your car you may risk losing $95,000? What about $75,000 or $25,000? If your answer is yes, I can sleep at night, you have a high risk tolerance. If your answer is no, I am absolutely, uncomfortable knowing the majority of my assets are at risk when I drive my car everyday, your risk tolerance is low. Or perhaps you are somewhere in the middle. How much risk can you withstand?

You may find yourself thinking deeply about your sleep factor if you are a commuter or a road warrior who does a lot of business travel in your car. When traveling the interstate frequently, you are likely to see or hear about collisions daily or you had a near miss a time or two. What if you caused a multi vehicle collision with major casualties? From a financial standpoint, what will be your game plan for the worst case scenario?

Risk tolerance is yours. You own it. If you decide to assume some risk and are able to sleep at night, take ownership of your decision to do so. Risk tolerance goes beyond the value of your assets; it stretches into the worst case scenario zone. Weigh in on the answers to why you are going to take on the risk as well as the potential consequence.

Worst Case Scenarios

Scenario #1:

What if you are found responsible for a major automobile accident causing multiple casualties and the court enters a judgment against you to pay $350,000 in excess of your auto policy's liability limits? For starters virtually everything you own will be fair game to pay your financial obligation. Did you know, if you do not have enough wealth to satisfy the judgment your future earnings and assets can be seized?

Scenario #2

What if you collide with a hit and run driver?

Scenario #3

What if you were in an accident with a driver who is underinsured or even worse uninsured? If you do not have uninsured/underinsured liability coverage on your auto policy, more than likely you will need to use your "own" money to pay for any medical expenses, car repairs, or replace your vehicle. You can take the at fault driver to court for these damages. But the court process takes time. In the short term, you will need to take care of your health and car situation. Your money reserves will be tapped for sure in the interim unless; the uninsured at fault driver has the means to repay you. Worst case scenario the underinsured or uninsured driver at fault may be broke.

Other Basic Features of Auto Insurance You Need To Know

Features and coverage of auto policies vary amongst insurance companies. Nonetheless, most auto insurance companies will offer six basic components of an auto insurance policy:

1. **Bodily Injury Liability:** This coverage pays for "pain and suffering." It covers bodily injuries caused by you or family members listed on your policy.

2. **Property Damage Liability:** Covers any damages to a vehicle, public property, real estate or other structures hit by your car.

3. **Uninsured/Underinsured Liability:** When you are in an accident with an at fault driver who does not have adequate split limits of liability coverage or no car insurance at all, this coverage pays your claims. This also applies to hit and run drivers or protecting you financially if you are hit as a pedestrian.

4. **Comprehensive Coverage:** Pays for damages to your vehicle that did not involve an auto accident. (i.e. fire, vandalism, theft, disasters like storms, hurricanes, trees falling on your car).

5. **Collision Coverage:** Whether you are at fault or you're not at fault, this coverage pays for damage to your car as a result of a collision with another vehicle. In the event you are not at fault, the insurance company will recoup the claim paid to you from the other driver's insurance company.

6. **Personal Injury Protection (a.k.a. P.I.P):** Covers medical payments, lost wages to the policyholder or any passengers in

the vehicle when the collision took place. Coverage may also cover the cost of funeral services.

Common Car Insurance Riders (Add-ons)

Auto insurance companies also offer additional optional "supplemental" benefits that you can add to your policy. These are known as policy riders. Policy riders are optional types of coverage that may be added to your basic insurance policy and usually requires an additional premium payment. You can expand your protection by adding optional benefits that you can rely on when you need it most.

Three most common riders available are:

- **Towing and labor coverage:** This is your personal road side assistance plan and covers the cost of emergency car services needed to repair a flat tire or tow your vehicle if it breaks down.

- **Rental reimbursement coverage:** If your car is stolen, in the repair shop for a claim related incident, or totaled, this coverage offers the option to rent a car for a specified period of time so that you can continue your daily activities while seeking a permanent solution to replace your vehicle.

- **Gap automobile insurance coverage:** Gap insurance is coverage for people who are leasing or financing their vehicle. It provides protection if your car is totaled and is worth less than your outstanding loan or remaining lease amount due. If you owe more than the car is worth, you are said to be "upside down". If your vehicle is totaled in an accident, your insurance company will only pay you the book value of the car not what is still owed on it. Gap insurance is a solution for this situation. It pays, "the gap," between the book value and the full amount owed on the car. Otherwise your finance company will expect you to pay out of pocket for the shortfall.

> ## YOUR FINANCIAL FITNESS WORKOUT:
> ### Weigh In Auto Insurance

Now that you know your approach to putting auto insurance in place is not only about replacing your car or being able to payoff the finance company if your car is totaled, put your personal interests first. Which policy limits and features of auto insurance are best for you?

This financial workout will guide you to:

- Focus on your personal interests when choosing auto insurance.
- Become familiar with your existing auto policy.
- Consult with an insurance professional with a list of questions to ask.

For this workout you will need a copy of your auto insurance policy. If you do not have a current copy handy, call your auto insurer and request a copy be mailed, faxed, or sent via e-mail to you. Your insurer may also make your policy available for viewing online. Also, I've provided a worksheet located at the end of this section that you can use along with this workout.

Step One: Evaluate Your Personal Interests

When evaluating your personal interests there are three points to consider.

1. **Total Value of Your Assets**

    In Section I. on the worksheet, record the total value of your assets. Revisit your net worth statement to get this number.

2. **Risk Tolerance**

    Ask yourself the following questions:

    - How would I feel if I had to use 100% of my assets to pay for automobile related claims and court ordered judgments?
    - What if I had to pay using 25%-50% of my assets?

    Hone in on your sleep factor. Risk tolerance is yours. You own it. If you decide to assume some risk and are able to sleep at night, take ownership of your decision to do so. Risk tolerance goes beyond the value of your assets; it stretches into the worst case scenario zone. Weigh in on the answers to why you are going to take on the risk as well as the potential consequence.

3. **Worst Case Scenario:**

    Give the possibility for a worst case scenario some thought. Are you interested in extra protection (coverage) so that you can plan for worst case scenario?

- What if you caused a major collision with claims in excess of $200,000?
- What if a drivers hits you then runs?
- What if your car was totaled and your car just happened to be "upside down?"
- What if…..you fill in the blank?

Step Two: Become Familiar with Your Auto Policy Limits and Premiums

How familiar are you with the coverage details of your existing policy?

The benefits of this exercise are:

- Becoming familiar with your existing auto insurance policy.
- Determining whether your coverage meets your lifestyle needs.
- Having your policy's coverage outlined so that when you begin shopping auto insurance rates, you will have a basis for comparison.
- Getting in touch with the itemized premiums you are paying for coverage.

If you have no auto insurance, use this worksheet as a guide when you are shopping for coverage.

Section I: Assets, Liabilities, and GAP

1. On page 125, record the book value of your vehicle. You can research the value at www.nadaguides.com. N.A.D.A. is the

automotive industry's official guide to new and used vehicle pricing for all makes and models.

2. List current balance of your auto loan.

3. Calculate your gap, if any. Subtract book value from loan value.

Section II. Auto Coverage

Review your existing policy and list policy limits, deductible, and premiums for coverage you selected. Include any optional coverage not listed.

Section III. Riders

List any riders added to the policy along with coverage details/limits and premiums.

Does your existing policy match up with your personal interests, risk tolerance, and consideration for worst case scenario? If your answer is no, consult with an auto insurance professional and consider making changes to your policy that meet your lifestyle needs.

Step Three: Consult with an Insurance Professional

You've become reacquainted with your existing auto policy; share your discovery with an insurance professional and be sure your coverage is a good match for your lifestyle. An insurance professional can help you clarify your needs, exposure to risk, and offer guidance when choosing auto policy features. Their role is helping you choose coverage that is suitable for your lifestyle and spending plan.

When consulting a professional regarding any type of insurance plan, always have an idea of how much money is available in your spending plan to finance the coverage. Decide whether you are open to making premium payments monthly, quarterly, semi-annual or annually? Also, be proactive and ask questions about how the insurance plan works and what factors influence your premiums.

Here's a list of questions that you can ask to gain a deeper understanding about auto insurance coverage and premiums.

1. What are the basic policy features and available coverage limits? What additional riders can be added on and what do they cover?

2. Does the insurance company offer any discounts? Is there a discount available if both my home and car are insured with the same company? Is there a multiple car discount?

3. What are my premium payment options? Is there a way to lower my premiums?

4. What factors increase a policy cost? How does my driving history affect my auto insurance rates?

5. Will everyone in my household be covered? If I allow other licensed drivers to drive my car are they covered?

6. What are the state's liability insurance requirements for new or used cars?

7. I use my car for business, is it covered under my policy?

8. What situations will not be covered by my auto insurance coverage?

9. What is the length of time that the policy is in effect? What can result in the policy being cancelled or an increase in premiums?

10. If I have a lower deductible, how much are my payments? With a higher deductible what are the premiums?

Step Four: Shop Around

One way to know whether you are getting the coverage you need or affordable premiums for auto insurance is to shop around. It is okay to shop around for auto insurance anytime to make sure you are getting the best coverage at a premium you can afford. Then too, there are specific instances when you should invest the time to shop around for the best possible rates. For example:

- **Your current auto insurance policy is coming up for renewal.**

    It is common for consumers to compare auto insurance rates at time of renewal. You may be able to save money if another insurance company can beat your current rate.

- **Your existing auto policy's rates increased or decreased.**

    A good time to shop around for auto insurance is when your premiums increased; maybe you will be able to find a lower rate. Did you know it is also a good time to shop around if your auto insurance rates decreased? If your auto insurance company lowered your premiums chances are other insurers are lowering premiums too. This will be a good time to see if you may find an insurer that can offer you an even lower rate.

- **You're moving.**

    A change in your ZIP code may also result in a change in your auto insurance rates. Auto insurance rates notably vary within cities, states, urban and rural areas. If you change your residence, consider comparing auto insurance premiums to be sure you are getting the best coverage and lowest rate available.

- **You're buying a new car.**

    Compare auto insurance rates to see which insurers can offer you the best rate based on your new vehicle.

- **You're getting married.**

    If there is more than one vehicle insured under the same policy many insurers will offer a discount referred to as a multi-car discount. If you and your new spouse each have a car and decide to cover your vehicles under one auto policy, shop around for auto insurance that gives you the best rates that include a multi-car auto insurance discount.

- **You're buying a home.**

    Most insurance companies offer a "multi-line discount" if you insure your home or condo and car with them. If you have a home or condo, or are planning to purchase one, shop around for insurance companies that give you the best rates which also include a multi-line insurance discount on your auto and homeowner's insurance policy.

Chapter 6: Weigh In: Protect What You Value

SECTION I. Assets, Liabilities, and GAP	
Your Total Assets:	$_____
Book Value of Vehicle	$_____
If Financing or Leasing Vehicle, calculate GAP:	
Outstanding Loan Balance	$_____
(minus) Book Value of Car:	— $_____
(equals) GAP:	= $_____

SECTION II. Auto Coverage		Premium
Split Limits of Liability	____/____/____	$_____
Deductible	$_____	
Collision Coverage Split Limits	____/____/____	$_____
Deductible	$_____	
Comprehensive Coverage Amount	$_____	$_____
Deductible	$_____	
Uninsured/Underinsured Split Limits	____/____/____	$_____
Medical Payment Coverage Personal Injury Protection	$_____	$_____

SECTION III. Riders		
ex. Gap Coverage	$_____	$_____
ex. Towing and Labor		$_____
ex. Rental Reimbursement	$_____	$_____
	Total Premium	$_____

Weigh In: Personal Umbrella Liability Insurance

Personal "Umbrella" liability insurance is a lot like its name. It can be a "personal financial umbrella" for a financial storm. It is commonly known as a second layer of supplemental liability protection that may protect you from having to use your assets to pay excessive accident related claims. The two key words to remember about umbrella insurance are "supplemental" and "liability." Umbrella policies supplement the liability limits of your auto, renters, and homeowners insurance. This means it offers additional insurance protection that kicks in once you exhaust the liability limits of your auto, renter's and homeowner's insurance policies. It is typically sold in expansive increments of $1,000,000 with an average inexpensive premium of $150-$250 per year. A personal umbrella policy not only protects you; if your family members or pets unintentionally cause an accident, they are covered also.

Example #1: Supplementing Auto Insurance

A driver is responsible for an automobile accident and the court ordered the driver to pay $300,000 in damages to the casualties for bodily injuries. However, the maximum amount the auto insurance company will pay on the behalf of the driver is $100,000. If the driver has a personal umbrella policy, it can be used as supplemental liability insurance and kick in to pay the S200,000 difference after the auto insurance company pays its share. Otherwise, without an umbrella policy, the driver will be responsible for paying the claim's excess out of pocket.

Example #2: Supplementing Homeowners Insurance

Suppose the pizza delivery man slips on your icy drive way, your dog bites the landscaper, there is a fire on your rental property that spreads to neighboring units or the neighbor's children get hurt in your pool? What if the current liability limits of your homeowners insurance is inadequate to protect you financially? A personal umbrella policy can take over and provide an additional layer of liability coverage that can shelter you from a financial storm, worst case scenario.

No matter how careful you try to be, accidents happen. An accident can take place on your property, or you may cause an accident and injure someone or destroy someone's property away from home. A victim may hire an aggressive attorney to file a lawsuit against you. Just know the attorney is coming for the biggest bite of your assets that can legally be taken away from you. If you do not have enough liability coverage to pay for the lawsuit, the hungry attorney will seek your future income.

Carrying personal umbrella insurance protection is a new concept for most people. It is also the most overlooked insurance coverage often not found in a person's insurance portfolio. Perhaps it is missing from most people's portfolio because the misconception about umbrella insurance is that it is only necessary for people who have millions of dollars of wealth at stake. Not true. Umbrella liability insurance benefits are for anyone who values their financial security and desires to protect it. The only prerequisite to obtain umbrella liability insurance is having a minimum level of liability limits already in place on auto, renters or homeowners policies. This makes sense because umbrella insurance is designed to kick in where other liability coverage ends.

Personal Umbrella Policy Exclusions

Of all of the insurance plans suggested for your insurance portfolio, umbrella insurance will more than likely be the simplest coverage to understand. What you should remember most about personal umbrella policies are the details regarding any exclusions listed in the policy.

Insurance policy exclusions are items specifically not covered in a policy. Policy exclusions vary among insurance companies. Before purchasing umbrella insurance, ask the insurance company what are the standard policy exclusions? This way you won't be caught off guard and learn the damages are not covered when you are seeking to file a claim; or most of all you want a policy that is suitable for you. Some insurers will offer the opportunity to buy additional coverage for the stated exclusions so that you can add the protection to your policy. These additions are called policy endorsements. You can determine whether additional endorsements are beneficial based on your personal interests.

> **YOUR FINANCIAL FITNESS WORKOUT:**
> **Weigh In Umbrella Liability Insurance**

There's nothing like experiencing the peace of mind that comes with knowing you have financial protection just in case something catastrophic happens. It is not uncommon in today's society to hear of lawsuit settlements that exceed $300,000. The average auto, renters, and home insurance policyholders carry liability limits from $100,000-$300,000. Unless you have an umbrella policy, you may need more liability coverage than you think. But of course, it all depends on your risk tolerance. Consider adding personal umbrella insurance to your insurance portfolio.

This financial workout will guide you to:

- Focus on your personal interests when considering an umbrella policy.
- Become familiar with your existing auto, renters or homeowner's liability limits.
- Consult with an insurance professional.

For this workout you will need a copy of your auto, renters or homeowner's policies. If you do not have a current copy handy, call your insurer and request a copy be mailed, faxed, or sent via e-mail to you. Your insurer may also make your policy available for viewing online.

Step One: Evaluate Your Personal Interests

As with all insurance plans, your initial approach to purchasing insurance is evaluating your personal interests. Here are some points to consider for personal umbrella insurance.

- Count your pennies. Have you consider the value of all your assets.
- What is your risk tolerance?
- What is the total amount of liability coverage on your auto, renters or homeowner's policies? Do you need more protection?

- Do you entertain guests frequently? Is alcohol involved?
- Do you own a pool, recreation area, or utilities like jet skis, boats, etc?
- Are you a long-distance commuter? Do you have long rides to and from work? Do you take road trips often?
- Do you have teenagers who are driving?

Umbrella insurance does more than protect you from claims and large settlements, umbrella insurance will pay attorney fees and court costs even if you are defending yourself in a frivolous lawsuit. Consider worst case scenario when answering the questions we just went through. Given the amount of protection that you will receive, umbrella policies are relatively inexpensive.

Step Two: Become Familiar with Liability Limits of Your Existing Policies

Become familiar with the liability limits of your existing auto, renters or homeowners policies. This is your first layer of liability protection. Your first line of defense for any liable claims against you will be your first layer of liability protection. From here based on your personal interests and lifestyle, weigh in on adding a second layer of liability protection—personal umbrella liability insurance to your insurance portfolio.

On the worksheet, list the liability limits of your auto, renters or homeowners policies.

Is your first layer of coverage aligned with your personal interests including your risk tolerance? Would an extra layer of liability protection give you peace of mind?

Step Three: Consult with an Insurance Professional

Having an insurance professional as one of your trusted advisors is recommended for everyone's lifestyle. It is no different than having a trusted primary care physician, dentist, or law professional whom you can rely on. A trusted insurance professional can recommend and guide you into the appropriate insurance plans for your insurance portfolio. The ideal scenario would be to seek the counsel of an insurance professional who is able to offer multiple lines of insurance such as auto, home, renters and personal umbrella insurance. Moreover, consider working with an insurance professional who works with a reputable insurance company.

There are benefits of working with an insurance professional who can offer multiple lines of insurance. For example:

- The insurance professional will have an opportunity to conduct a holistic needs analysis based on various areas of your lifestyle and then integrate lines of insurance protection tailored to your scenario.
- You may be entitled to a multiple line discount if you purchase more than one line of insurance from an insurance professional.
- You can have an insurance professional who is familiar with you whom you can call on for advice and direction when you experience changes in your lifestyle.

How to Meet an Insurance Professional

The best way to meet an insurance professional is by way of a recommendation from a trusted family member or friend. If a professional is highly recommended, there is a good chance that person will offer you a valuable service too.

Another way to meet an insurance professional is by calling a reputable insurance company and requesting a face-face initial consultation to discuss your need for protection. In this case, you will have an opportunity to interview a professional and determine if the person's personality and product offerings will be a good fit for you.

When choosing a reputable insurance company, consider a company with an insurance rating that demonstrates they are financially sound. Consumers rely on insurance companies to deliver on their promises to pay claims; the insurance industry has agencies that rate a company's financial reputation and ability to do so. To research a reputable company and their rating go to www.ambest.com. Then, request an initial consultation with insurance companies rated A+ or A++ by the A.M. Best Company.

Step Four: Shop Around

Shop around. Always shop around for the best rates or multiple line discounts. Your key points to compare when shopping umbrella insurance coverage are:

- Minimum liability limits needed on auto, home, or renter's insurance
- Policy coverage details
- Liability limits
- Premiums

Chapter 6: Weigh In: Protect What You Value 131

- Deductible
- Policy exclusions
- Multiple line discounts

The comparison shopper guide on the worksheet will help you keep notes and stay on track when you are shopping around.

Ask the following questions about umbrella insurance when meeting with an insurance professional:

1. What does the policy cover? What coverage amounts are available?
2. Does the insurance company offer a multiple line discount?
3. What are my premium payment options?
4. What factors increase a policy's cost?
5. How do I ensure my household members and pets are covered?
6. What are the minimum liability insurance requirements that I must carry on my car, home or renters insurance?
7. Do you offer worldwide coverage?
8. What situations will not be covered by my umbrella policy? Name the policy's exclusions.
9. What is the length of time that the policy is in effect?
10. Can I be turned down for coverage? What can result in the policy being cancelled or an increase in premiums?

Personal Umbrella Insurance Protects You and Your Family

Type of Insurance	Limits of Liability	Type of Coverage
Ex. Auto	$100/300/100	Uninsured/Underinsured
Auto	$_____	
Auto	$_____	
Renters	$_____	
Homeowners	$_____	

Comparison Shopper Guide

Minimum Liability Limits Needed to Carry on Auto	$_____/_____/_____
Minimum Liability Limits Needed to Carry on Renters or Home	$_____
Umbrella Coverage Amount	$_____/_____/_____
List Policy Exclusions:	
	Premium $_____

Chapter 6: Weigh In: Protect What You Value

Weigh In: Homeowner's Insurance

This section offers the basics about homeowners insurance. Your real estate is one of the single largest investments that you'll own. If you own a home or rental property, chances are it comprises a significant portion of your net worth. Not knowing how homeowner's insurance policies are designed to protect you can cause some very unpleasant surprises financially particularly when you need to file a claim.

Often times consumers first and last contact with their homeowner's insurance policy was at the mortgage closing. Knowing they satisfied their commitment to fulfill the mortgage bank's interests, they file the policy away on a wing and prayer that they will not ever need to use it. Since the policy is filed away and more than likely never looked at again, it is possible the consumer may lose touch with what type of coverage and policy limits they actually have. Worst case scenario, their home has appreciated in value, yet their home's insurance coverage has not.

When implementing homeowners insurance in your portfolio, your priorities are to protect:

- The fair market value of the structure of your home.
- The ability to rebuild another home of the same value if yours is destroyed.
- The value of the personal contents of your home.
- The home's equity from law suit related claims.

Q&A: You Need To Know Your Answers

1. What is the coverage limit for the structure of your home? If your home was destroyed by a natural disaster, do you have

enough insurance coverage to build another home of the same value?

2. What are the coverage limits for the personal contents of your home? Does the insurance company have an inventory listing of your valued personal belongings?

3. Will your homeowners insurance policy pay structure and personal property claims according to the "Actual Cash Value" or "Replacement Cost?"

Your home is your sanctuary. As your cherished refuge, it provides enormous value emotionally and financially. In a different way, so does real estate investment property. It is likely your real estate is one of the stakes in your wealth building plan to achieve financial freedom. You need to know the answers to the questions above and have an acceptable understanding of how homeowner's insurance policies are designed. It is so important to evaluate your homeowners insurance year to year and protect your ability to replace your home, its contents and your wealth, worst case scenario. If you ever find yourself in the position to rebuild the structure of your home or replace its contents and you are underinsured, you may suffer in a financial way and instantly lose your real estate equity too.

Four Basic Coverage Components of Homeowners Insurance

Homeowners insurance is designed to include four basic coverage components:

- Structure "Dwelling" Coverage
- Personal Property Coverage
- Liability Coverage
- Temporary Displacement Compensation

Structure

Dwelling coverage insures the structural build of your home which also includes detached structures such as a garage, barn, gazebos, sheds etc. This coverage insures your home against damages caused by common perils. A list of common perils unless otherwise noted in your policy as excluded may include:

- Fire
- Theft, vandalism, and mischief
- Accidental damage from smoke
- Extreme weather, lightening, snow, ice, hurricanes etc.
- Frozen plumbing, water damage due to plumbing
- Objects falling from the sky

Your policy will indicate which types of perils are excluded from covering your home's structure. For example, flood damage is usually excluded from standard policies. If you live in a flood zone or near large bodies of water, flood coverage may be important to you. You can add flood coverage protection and other excluded perils by purchasing an endorsement to your policy.

Endorsements are optional agreements which may alter the provisions of a standard insurance policy. Endorsements allow you to obtain additional insurance with separate coverage limits for perils that are otherwise excluded from your policy, increase policy limits for personal property, or endorse protecting property that may be excluded from a standard policy.

Personal Property

Personal property protection covers the personal contents of your home. This would include furnishings, jewelry, and high ticket items such as furs, art, and collectibles. If your personal valuables are damaged or stolen, whether or not the activity occurred on or off the premises of your home, you are covered. It is important to note however, these general guidelines hold true for most homeowner's insurance policies. Yet, there is a variance of coverage limits, perils, and exclusions among insurance companies for certain types of personal property.

Typically, the same perils for structure coverage are considered for personal property. As with most policies for an additional premium, you can increase your coverage limits or include personal property that may be otherwise excluded by adding endorsements.

Liability

The standard amount of liability coverage for most home insurance policies is $100,000. By now after reading about auto and personal umbrella insurance, you should have a pretty good understanding of the way you benefit from liability protection. Ask yourself, does your personal interests require more or less than $100,000 of liability protection coverage?

Liability coverage of your homeowner's policy is your first line of defense to protect you from claims for negligence. It is also expansive and protects you and your household members from any liable claims for accidents that takes place on or off your property. A little known fact about homeowner's liability insurance--it can be used to supplement auto insurance liability limits as well.

Temporary Displacement Coverage

If you experience damages to your home and you are unable to inhabit your residence temporarily, this coverage will compensate you for the costs of temporary housing, basic living expenses, food and clothing. The benefits are tied to time dependent guidelines and coverage limits. Coverage options vary among insurance companies. Inquire about exclusions.

Homeowner's Insurance "Pay-Out" Methods

Question: Will your homeowners insurance policy pay structure and personal property claims according to the "**Actual Cash Value**" or "**Replacement Cost?**"

Having the answers to which type of perils, exclusions, and coverage limits are endorsed in your homeowners policy is half the battle. Knowing the compensation method for structure and personal property claims you are subject to receive is the crucial other half.

Insurance companies endorse in your homeowners policy one of two compensation methods to calculate reimbursement for a loss or damage to your home's structure or personal property—actual cash value or replacement cost. You choose the "pay-out" method when you purchase the policy.

Actual Cash Value Method

The actual cash value method compensates you for claims based on your coverage limits after deducting depreciation. Depreciation is expressed as the decrease in value of your home's structure or personal property due to age, condition of property, and normal wear and tear.

For example:

Your home is 9 years old and a storm damages your roof. It is going to cost $20,000 to replace it. According to the actual cash value method, the insurance company will deduct depreciation. (condition, age, normal wear and tear) from $20,000 and pay you the difference. Then you are responsible for paying your contractor out of pocket for the remaining balanced owed.

Replacement Cost Coverage

Replacement cost coverage pays claims for the full amount based on the coverage limits in your policy. Provided you replace or repair your home or personal property with materials of similar kind and quality, the insurance company will pay 100 percent of the claim without deducting for depreciation. This way you can replace the damaged or personal property loss with a new one of similar quality and value.

Replacement cost compensation saves you the burden of having to pay out of pocket to supplement the expense for replacing or repairing your property. Having assurance you will be financially protected fully within your policy limits helps to ease the moments of bewilderment associated with unfortunate losses.

Proof of Claim: Inventory Your Personal Property

Keeping an inventory of your personal property along with receipts and appraisals will serve you best so that you can show proof of payment for reimbursement when filing a claim. Learn your insurer's procedure for filing claims for losses and damages before purchasing coverage. This way you know what documentation and proof of purchases you will need to have on record so that you can maximize the use of your coverage and the services of the insurance company.

To insure your personal belongings properly, you can submit a personal inventory list of items to be considered for protection to the insurance company. In addition to your list, submit purchase receipts, pictures, and/or videos, and appraisals of jewelry, art and collectibles. Then store a copy for yourself in a safe place away from you home, ideally a safe deposit box. Often after a fire, theft, or accident takes place, no one can recall all of the personal belongings they owned or how much they paid for them when filing for a claim. Filing an inventory listing of your personal belongings with the insurance company and placing a copy in your safe deposit box can be a "savings" grace in more ways than one.

> **YOUR FINANCIAL FITNESS WORKOUT:**
> **Weigh In Homeowner's Insurance**

Step One: Evaluate Your Personal Interests

Evaluate:

- The value of your real estate and personal contents.
- Your risk tolerance
- Worst case scenario

Here are a few questions for you to think through if you have homeowner's insurance:

1. When was the last time you appraised your home?
2. Have you upgraded your home adding value to your real estate? If so, consider reviewing your home insurance and increase coverage for the structure of your home based on the present market value with the upgrades.
3. What is the compensation method endorsed in your policy?

Here are a few points to consider in general or if you are planning to purchase insurance for your home:

1. Insuring your home based on the mortgage loan balance may not be sufficient protection. The value of your real estate and cost to rebuild it if destroyed by fire or other natural disaster may be worth more than the actual loan balance.
2. Which perils are included or excluded?
3. What are the standard policy exclusions?
4. What is the value of the personal contents of your home?
5. What are the policy limits for replacing personal property?
6. Do you need additional endorsements for luxury property such as furs, engagement rings, jewelry, watches, antiques, art or other excluded property?
7. What limits for liability insurance is suitable for your risk tolerance?
8. Which compensation method is agreeable to you—actual cash value or replacement cost?
9. What is the process for filing claims and documentation needed for reimbursement?
10. What are the guidelines for filing temporary displacement compensation claims?

Step Two: Become Familiar with Your Existing Policy

If you have homeowners insurance this exercise will guide you to become familiar with the details of your policy using the worksheet at the end of the workout. For this exercise you will need a copy of your homeowner's insurance policy. Get your copy in hand and follow

Chapter 6: Weigh In: Protect What You Value   141

along the next steps to record the details of your policy. At the end of the exercise evaluate whether or not your policy' coverage is a good fit for your personal interests and coverage needs.

If you are planning to buy homeowners insurance or shop around, the worksheet can also be used as a tool when comparison shopping.

Record the following details:
1. Record the structure coverage limit stated in your policy.
2. Record the policy's premium for structure coverage.
3. List the appraised value of your home, date of appraisal and current market cost to rebuild the structure. A real estate agent can offer assistance in helping you obtain an appraisal so that you can evaluate the fair market value of your real estate. The agent can also provide an analysis of the cost to rebuild based on the current costs for home construction in your city.

Homeowner's Insurance Policy	Amount of Coverage	Premium
I. Structure Coverage	$_____	$_____
Appraised Value of Your Home	$_____	
Date of Appraisal	___/___/___	
Cost to Rebuild Structure	$_____	

Is the structure of your home underinsured or adequately covered? As the value of your home increases and the costs to rebuild homes in your zip code fluctuates, update your homeowner's insurance accordingly. Review your homeowner's policy year to year to be sure you are protecting your personal interests.

Endorsements, Perils, and Exclusions of Structure Coverage

1. List any endorsements you've added to the structure coverage. List each endorsement and the coverage limits on the worksheet individually.
2. List premiums for added endorsements.
3. List included and excluded perils.

Home Insurance Policy	Coverage Limits	Premium
I. Structure Coverage		
List Endorsements Added	$_____	$_____
List Included Perils		
List Excluded Perils		

Are you comfortable with the excluded perils? Or would you prefer to alter the standard policy and add endorsements?

Weigh In: Personal Property Coverage

1. List the value of he personal contents of your home.
2. List the coverage limits for Personal Property as stated in your policy. (itemize where applicable)
3. List any endorsements for personal property.
4. List included and excluded perils.
5. List the premiums for coverage and endorsements.

Luxury items like furs, engagement rings, and watches may have specific individual coverage limits. You may need to add endorsements to fully insure luxury items.

Home Insurance Policy	Coverage Limits	Premium
II. Personal Property Coverage	$_____	$_____
Value of Personal Contents of Home	$_____	
List Endorsements Added	$_____	$_____
List Included Perils		
List Excluded Perils		

Often times, personal property coverage is overlooked by consumers. Typically, they underestimate the value of the contents of their home. Take a look around your home. At a glance, do you feel you have enough coverage for your furniture, and other items in your home?

Does the thought of adding up the value of the contents of the home overwhelm you? Don't let it. Just simply take it one room at a time. Go into each room of your home and inventory the contents and the value of what you paid for the items. It may take a little time to complete but it will be worth protecting the value of your cherished "pieces."

Then stack up the value of your content against the coverage limits of your policy. Are your personal valuables fully insured? If not, you can consider increasing the coverage limits or adding endorsements.

Liability Coverage

Your homeowner's policy gives you the opportunity to extend liability protection to your household family members. Consider their assets as well as yours when assessing how much liability coverage to carry. Ideally, you are protecting their financial well being too. Most of all, verify the insurance company has your family members listed on your policy for protection.

On the worksheet list the liability coverage as stated in your policy. List the assets of your household members. Are you fully insured or underinsured? Does your coverage include extra padded protection for worst case scenarios? What is your sleep factor?

Home Insurance Policy	Coverage Limits	Premium
III. Liability Coverage	$_____	$_____

Household Member	Total Assets
You	$_____
Spouse	$_____
Child	$_____
Child	$_____
Grand Total Assets	$_____

Compensation Method

Review your policy and record the compensation method that will be used for reimbursement of claims. Is it actual cash value or replacement cost? Are you comfortable with your pay out method? If not, inquire about making a change.

Step Three: Shop Around

Shop until you drop for the best rates of reputable financially sound insurance companies. Your trusted resource for researching a company's profile is www.ambest.com.

Additionally, take note of <u>five ways</u> to lower your homeowner's insurance premiums.

1. **Shop Around.** Don't just take price into consideration. Also, assess the company's financial stability and quality of service.

2. **Raise Your Deductible.** The higher the deductible, the lower the premiums.
3. **Buy Auto and Home Insurance from the Same Insurance Company.** Most insurance companies offer a multi-line discount.
4. **Install a Home Security System.** Insurance companies offer discount for smoke detectors, dead bolt locks, sophisticated sprinkler systems, and fire & burglar alarms that alerts the fire department, police, or other security monitoring stations.
5. **Maintain a Good Credit Report.** The pulse of your credit score matters when purchasing homeowner's insurance. Insurers are increasingly using credit reports to quote insurance premiums. A favorable credit history can lower your premiums.

Homeowner's Insurance Policy	Amount of Coverage	Premium
I. Structure Coverage	$	$
Appraised Value of Your Home	$	
Date of Appraisal	___/___/___	
Cost to Rebuild Structure	$	
List Endorsements Added	$	$
List Included Perils		
List Excluded Perils		
Total Premium for Structure		$

Chapter 6: Weigh In: Protect What You Value

Home Insurance Policy	Coverage Limits	Premium
II. Personal Property Coverage	$_____	$_____
Value of Personal Contents of Home	$_____	
List Endorsements Added	$_____	$_____
List Included Perils		
List Excluded Perils		
Total Premium for Personal Property		$_____

Home Insurance Policy	Coverage Limits	Premium
III. Liability Coverage	$_____	$_____
Household Member	**Total Assets**	
You	$_____	
Spouse	$_____	
Child	$_____	
Child	$_____	
Grand Total Assets	$_____	
Total Premium for Liability		$_____
IV. Compensation Method		
Total Policy Premium		$_____

Weigh In: Renter's Insurance

Most people who are renting a residence have not given thought to "insuring their home." Although you are not the owner of the property, you have the value of personal possessions in your home to protect. What happens when your clothing, furniture, and state of the art audio equipment are ruined because the tenants upstairs flooded their unit and yours too? Or heaven forbid you are burglarized? It can be very expensive to replace personal belongings that you worked so hard to obtain.

Did you know rental insurance can protect your financial security and pay for temporary living expenses in a hotel or other rental if your apartment is damaged or lost due to a fire or other perils outlined in your policy. Your landlord's homeowner's insurance will more than likely repair any damage to your unit but will not "replace" your treasured personal property or help you financially to get situated in a new living arrangement if necessary.

A renter's policy protects your property from named perils outlined in your coverage. These usually include fire or lightning, windstorm or hail, explosions, riots, vehicles, smoke, vandalism or malicious mischief, theft, falling objects, extreme weather, accidental discharge or overflow of water or steam, sudden and accidental damage from artificially generated electrical current, and more. Review your policy for details.

Consider adding rental insurance to your insurance portfolio. Personal liability insurance is also available through renters insurance policies. Request adding personal liability to your policy. It is not a standard feature.

Four Basic Components of Renter's Insurance

There are four basic components to renters insurance: personal property, additional living expenses, personal liability, and medical payments.

Personal Property

This offers protection for your personal property and contents of your home. Renters insurance coverage applies to your personal property no matter where you take it with you. The coverage limits are chosen by you when you purchase the policy. Standard renters insurance policies offer limited coverage for luxury items—typically maximum $1,000 for named perils. Additional endorsements to protect luxury items can be added to your policy.

Additional Living Expenses

In the event of an accident and your residence is seriously damaged, this coverage will cover additional expenses for you to live in a hotel or elsewhere for a period of time while your unit is being repaired. Inquire about coverage limits.

Personal Liability

Typically, personal liability coverage is not a standard feature of renters insurance. You must request that it be added to your policy. This coverage pays for any lawsuit claims against you for negligence caused by you while on or off your property. It also pays for your legal defense if you are sued based on specific situations listed in the policy. Know the inclusions and exclusion endorsed in the policy.

A major difference between renters insurance and homeowner's insurance is:

- Under most renter policies, personal liability coverage covers claims for bodily injury or property damage as long as it is not vehicle-related.
- Claims based on business activities are excluded too.

Medical Payments

This is not standard coverage but can be added for an additional premium. The policy normally includes limits of $1,000 per person.

Compensation Methods

As with any type of insurance coverage designed to pay you a benefit, awareness of the compensation method before you purchase the policy should be a high priority. You can choose how claims will be paid to you. Renter's insurance offers two compensation methods—"actual cash value" or "replacement cost" coverage.

Special Note: standard renter's policies cover personal property on an actual cash value basis. This means payments are based on the replacement cost of the property minus deductions for depreciation.

Replacement cost coverage can be added for an additional premium. With replacement coverage, insurance companies will pay one of the two amounts listed below, whichever is less:

- The cost to replace the property with property of a similar type and quality without a deduction for depreciation, or
- The full cost to repair item at the time of the loss.

Proof of Claim: Inventory Your Personal Property

Properly insure your personal belongings with your insurance company. Learn the insurance company's procedure for filing claims

Chapter 6: Weigh In: Protect What You Value   151

for damaged or stolen property and submit a personal inventory list of the contents of your home. Maintain purchase receipts, take pictures of your items, and/or videos, and obtain appraisals for jewelry, art and collectibles. Present copies to the insurance company; then store a copy for yourself in a safe deposit box. Often times following a burglary it may not be easy to recall everything that is missing. An inventory list of your personal belongings filed with the insurance company can serve as documentation that can help you with proof of any claims.

YOUR FINANCIAL FITNESS WORKOUT:
Weigh In Renter's Insurance

Renter's insurance is invaluable protection for your home. Plus, by adding liability insurance to your policy, you've invaluably protected your financial security. Weigh in on this coverage. It is relatively inexpensive. I am certain the value of the contents of your home and having the opportunity to protect your financial security is important to you. Get some quotes. Make it a goal to work the cost of renters insurance into your spending plan and protect what you value.

Step One: Evaluate Your Personal Interests

Points to consider and evaluate:

1. The value of the personal contents and valuables in your home.
2. Do you have roommates? Standard renter's policies cover only you and relatives who live with you. If your roommate is not a

relative, each of you will need your own renters policy to cover your own property and provide liability coverage for your own actions.

3. Adding endorsements:
   - Earthquake endorsement: Typically earthquakes are not covered on standard renters policies. If you live in an earthquake region, you may want to consider this coverage.
   - Computer endorsement: Broadens your coverage for computers by adding coverage for any peril unless otherwise noted in the policy.
   - Business pursuits endorsement: This endorsement extends your liability coverage to include protection against claims involving business pursuits.
   - Luxury items: fine jewelry, art, antiques, furs, collectibles etc.
4. Which perils are included or excluded?
5. Choosing a compensation method: Replacement value or actual cash value method.
6. How much liability coverage will be best for you?

Step Two: Become Familiar with your existing policy.

Follow my lead, become familiar with your existing policy by completing the worksheet at the end of the financial workout. You will need a current copy of your renter's policy. The worksheet can also be used as a tool when comparison shopping renter's insurance.

Personal Property Coverage

1. List the value of the personal contents of your home.
2. List the coverage limits for personal property as stated in your policy.
3. Individually list endorsements and specified coverage limits on the worksheet.
4. List included and excluded perils.
5. List the premium for coverage limits and endorsements.

Get reacquainted with the coverage limits for your personal property. For example, luxury items like furs, engagement rings, and watches may have limited coverage.

Renter's Insurance Policy	Coverage Limits	Premium
I. Personal Property Coverage	$_____	$_____
Value of Personal Contents of Home	$_____	
List Endorsements Added	$_____	$_____
List Included Perils		
List Excluded Perils		

Additional Living Expenses

1. List coverage limits for living expenses. List the premium.
2. List length of coverage. Typically additional living expense coverage is offered for a specified period of time.
3. List any exclusions associated with additional living expenses.

Does your coverage reflect your current lifestyle? Ideally you want enough protection that will give you the opportunity to occupy a home temporarily at a place that you will feel comfortable calling "my home." Give it some thought and protect maintaining your current style of living.

Renter's Insurance Policy	Coverage Limits	Premium
II. Additional Living Expenses	$_____	$_____
Length of coverage		
List Exclusions		

Liability Coverage

There are two important things to remember about liability coverage of renter's insurance:

- Typically, it is not a feature of the standard renters policy. You must request to have it endorsed.
- Under most renter's policies, liability coverage pays claims for bodily injury or property damage as long as it is not vehicle-

Chapter 6: Weigh In: Protect What You Value 155

related. To supplement your auto insurance liability coverage plus expand your lifestyle's financial protection, consider purchasing personal umbrella insurance.

1. List the liability coverage and premium as stated in your policy.
2. List the total value of your assets and any policy exclusions too.

Renter's Insurance Policy	Coverage Limits	Premium
III. Liability Coverage	$_____	$_____
Total Value of Assets	$_____	
List Exclusions		

Are you fully insured or underinsured? Do you feel a need for additional coverage?

Medical Payments

Medical payments are not a standard feature but can be added to your policy for an additional premium. It will come in handy if someone has an accident in your home. Many people like to entertain guests and enjoy dinner parties with cocktail hours. Accidents can happen, although your intention is to be sure everyone is joyful and safe. For an extra premium you can add this coverage and spare the out of pocket cost if someone gets hurt at your expense.

On the worksheet below, list your coverage limits per person for medical payments. List the premium and exclusions.

Renter's Insurance Policy	Coverage Limits	Premium
IV. Medical Payments Coverage Per Person	$_____	$_____
List Exclusions		

Compensation Method

Review your policy and record the compensation method that will be used for reimbursement of claims. Is it actual cash value or replacement cost?

Step Three: Shop Around

Shop around for the best rates. Inquire about multi-line discounts or other available discounts.

Additionally, take note of <u>five ways</u> to lower your renters insurance premiums.

1. **Shop Around.** Don't just take price into consideration. Also, assess the company's financial stability and quality of service.

There are specific instances when you should invest the time to shop around for the best possible rates.

- **Your current policy is coming up for renewal.**
- **You're moving.** A change in your ZIP code may result in a change in rates too.
- **You're buying a new car.** Most insurance companies offer a multi-line discount if you purchase both car and renters insurance.
- **You're getting married.** You can add your spouse to your policy. Plus, if there is more than one vehicle in your household and your car and renters insurance is with the same company, you may be entitled to a multi-line discount.

2. **Raise Your Deductible.** The higher the deductible, the lower the premiums.

3. **Buy Auto and Renter's Insurance from the Same Insurance Company.**

4. **Home Security Systems.** Insurance companies offer discount for smoke detectors, dead bolt locks, sophisticated sprinkler systems, and fire & burglar alarms that alerts the fire department, police, or other security monitoring stations.

5. **Maintain a Good Credit Report.** The pulse of your credit score matters when purchasing homeowner's insurance. Insurers are increasingly using credit reports to quote insurance premiums. A favorable credit history can lower your premiums.

Renter's Insurance Policy	Coverage Limits	Premium
I. Personal Property Coverage	$_____	$_____
Value of Personal Contents of Home	$_____	
List Endorsements Added	$_____	$_____
List Included Perils		
List Excluded Perils		
Total Premium for Personal Property:		$_____
II. Additional Living Expenses	$_____	$_____
Length of coverage	_____	
List Exclusions		
Total Premium for Living Expenses:		$_____
III. Liability Coverage	$_____	$_____
Total Value of Assets	$_____	
List Exclusions		
Total Premium for Liability:		$_____
IV. Medical Payments Coverage Per Person	$_____	$_____
List Exclusions		
Total Premium for Medical Payments:		$_____
V. Compensation Method	_____	
Total Policy Premium:		$_____

Weigh In: Life Insurance

Chances are you will live a long and healthy life providing for the needs of your lifestyle and the people you love. If you died tomorrow how would your loved ones make it financially? Would they be able to keep their standard of living without you?

When you lose someone you love, there is always an emotional struggle adjusting to life without them. Your loved ones emotional pain doesn't need to be coupled with financial woes. Protecting your loved ones with a sufficient amount of life insurance is a responsible and caring commitment. Having a sufficient amount of life insurance within your insurance portfolio ensures the people you love are taken care of financially when you are gone. Life insurance generally pays an income tax free financial benefit to your beneficiaries which can replace your income that is so needed by the people counting on you.

Do you need life insurance? If someone depends on you financially, you need life insurance. In my experience as a financial professional most people are not sure how much or what type of insurance product will be best for their needs. The most common questions asked are:

1. Do I need life insurance?
2. What is the right amount for me?
3. What are the different types of life insurance?
4. What type of life insurance should I buy?
5. Isn't what I have at work enough?

Up next, I will weigh in on the answers to the above questions to help you evaluate your need for life insurance coverage.

Weigh In: Do I Need Life Insurance?

Take note of the following specific instances that demonstrates a need for life insurance.

- **Everyone**

    Everyone needs life insurance to satisfy their responsibility for the final expenses of a proper burial. You wouldn't want your family to be burdened with paying for your funeral would you? Your family members are depending on you to be responsible and have a financial solution in place to provide for your special burial services. In today's dollars the average funeral cost will range from $10,000-$15,000 or more depending on the choice of funeral home and services, tombstone, or cemetery. Unless money is saved and set aside for final expenses, everyone needs life insurance to pay for their funeral.

- **Living Single**

    Too often single young people without children are told that they do not need life insurance because they do not have a family to worry about. I beg to differ. Everyone needs life insurance for funeral expenses. Also, there are single young people who provide financial support for aging parents, siblings, nieces or other immediate family members. If anyone depends on you financially, you need life insurance.

- **Living Married with Joint Income**

    The household of most married couples depends on two incomes to meet the needs for their family. If you suddenly died, would your family be able to maintain their standard of living in the absence of your income? Probably not. You can, however, provide for and protect them financially even if you are no longer living. Life insurance will provide tax free money to your family, replace your income and can help to financially sustain the people you love.

- **Single Parents**

  As a single parent you are the caregiver and sole breadwinner. With so much responsibility resting on your shoulders, and your children having only you to depend on, you want to be certain that you have enough life insurance coverage to safeguard your children's financial well being and future. Having life insurance can make a difference in ensuring your children goes to college and have an opportunity to succeed.

- **Stay-at-Home Parents**

  A stay at home parent brings a tremendous value and quality of life to the family. Just because stay at home parents aren't earning an income does not mean they don't contribute financially to the family and there is no need for life insurance. There are many important household activities stay at home parents perform that are often mistakenly underestimated:

  1. The family saves money that would otherwise be spent on childcare.
  2. Childcare, cooking, cleaning, chauffeuring the children to school, doctor visits, and after school activities are valuable.
  3 In fact, all of the activities of the stay at home parent have an economic value.

Consider life insurance for the stay at home parent to add financial protection which can help support the family and working spouse.

- **Spouse of the Stay at Home Parent**

    Working spouse answer the following questions:

    1. Could your spouse afford to continue staying at home unemployed without your income if you died?
    2. Could your spouse go back into the workforce, replace your exact income and afford the same lifestyle that you've provided for the family?

    Chances are the stay at home parent will not be able keep the family's lifestyle in tact as the working spouse did. If the working spouse dies and has not put enough life insurance in place, their family's lifestyle may change dramatically and cause them to suffer financially.

- **Your Legacy**

    In addition to caring for your loved ones' financial well being by carrying enough life insurance coverage, you may also be concerned about the well being of an organization that is near and dear to your heart. Life insurance can also be used as a charitable gift. Upon your death, you can bequeath a charitable contribution to your church, favorite non-profit or charity by naming the organization beneficiary of a life insurance policy. This is not a strategy only for "rich people." Anyone can give the gift of a charitable donation through the use of life insurance and create a lasting legacy.

Weigh In: What is The Right Amount For Me?

The answer is how much money does your family need when you are gone? Often, people arbitrarily choose a number for life insurance coverage like, $100,000, $250,000, or $1,000,000. I would say that is a good start but is it enough to preserve your loved ones standard of living over the long term? Is there a slight chance you arbitrarily chose a number out of the air for life insurance coverage like $250,000 without a true basis to back it up?

There is a simple approach to determine the amount of life insurance you may need. It is called a life insurance needs analysis. You are extraordinarily valuable to the people you love in more than an economic way. However, when you conduct a thorough life insurance needs analysis, you'll see the full picture of the economic impact you have on your family.

An analysis solves for three valuable needs for financial protection:

- Lump sum of money your family will need to pay off debts (i.e. mortgage, student loans, credit card debt, other loans and outstanding bills etc.)

- Lump sum needed to set aside for significant future expenses like college tuition or your funeral. See section I. of the chart on the next page.

- Lump sum of money needed to invest and create a reliable income stream to replace your income for a specific number of years. A life insurance needs analysis will take into account the current inflation rate and a projected before tax annual rate of return on the investment needed to help derive a reliable income. See section II. of the chart on the page 164.

I. Lump Sum Needed To Pay Off Debt/Expenses		II. Lump Sum Needed to Replace Income	
Final Expenses for Funeral	$15,000	Annual Income	$60,000
Debt excluding Mortgage	$48,000	Number of years to replace income	20
Mortgage	$189,000	Inflation	4.00%
College Funding	$300,000	Investment Rate of Return Before Tax	8%
Total Lump Sum Needed For Expenses:	**$552,000**	**Lump Sum Needed To Replace Income 20 years:**	**$1,050,291**

III. Offset Total Needed			
Income Replacement Needed	$1,050,291		
Lump Sum Debt/Expenses Needed	552,000		
Total Need For Financial Protection	**$1,602,291**	***Additional Life Insurance Needed:**	
Less Savings	-$7,000	**$1,321,291**	
Less Retirement fund	-$24,000		
Less 20 Yr Term Life Insurance	-$250,000		
Additional Life Insurance Needed	**$1,321,291**		

The established value of your total need for life insurance coverage is then offset by life insurance that you already have in place and other assets that you own such as savings, stocks, bonds, mutual funds, retirement accounts, real estate etc. See section III. of the chart on the previous page.

Weigh In: What are The Different Types of Life Insurance?

To simplify the answer, life insurance plans are placed in two categories commonly known as term or permanent insurance. There are various types of term and permanent life insurance plans in the marketplace. See examples of term and permanent insurance below.

TERM	PERMANENT
10 Year Term	Whole Life
20 Year Term	Universal Life
30 Year Term	Variable Universal Life

Term Insurance

Term insurance can be referred to as temporary insurance. Term insurance is typically offered for periods ranging from 1-30 years. When you buy term life insurance, you enter an agreement with the life insurance company to offer life insurance protection for a temporary time frame. For example a 10-year term life policy is life insurance coverage for ten years only. If you die during the coverage period, your beneficiaries will receive the life insurance proceeds. If you live beyond the coverage period, the agreement expires and the life insurance company will terminate the policy. However, prior to the policy's expiration, you always have the right to end the policy for any reason.

Term life insurance costs less than permanent coverage generally because it offers coverage for a temporary time frame. Because it is temporary coverage, term is generally recommended as a solution for short term financial protection needs. Typical short term financial protection includes covering a mortgage loan, other debts, or college tuition until paid in full or no longer a financial responsibility.

Permanent Insurance

Permanent life insurance can provide life long protection and is a viable solution for your long term financial protection needs. Long term needs may include providing for a family inheritance to heirs, leaving a lasting legacy to a charity, burial, to pay estate taxes, and replace retirement income for your living spouse. A unique feature of permanent life insurance that term life does not have is a cash value account. The cash value account is known as the living benefit of life insurance. The death benefit is what beneficiaries will receive when you die. The living benefit is your privilege to have access to take a distribution from the cash value of your life insurance while you are alive.

The cash value of life insurance policies accumulates and grows on a tax-deferred basis. Depending on the type of life insurance policy you choose, you may invest your cash value account at a fixed rate of interest as determined by the life insurance company. Or, you may invest your cash value in subaccounts that are tied to investments in the stock market. In addition to the primary purpose of the death benefit, policyholders may be attracted to the cash value benefit and use it as a tax favored savings vehicle to supplement their retirement income. Unlike traditional tax favored retirement plans you do not need to wait until you are age 59 to access your cash value account. Yet, there may be unique options or terms of your life insurance plan to follow when taking cash distributions.

There are three common types of permanent insurance policies:

- Whole Life
- Universal Life
- Variable Universal Life

Whole Life

Whole life insurance is a permanent life insurance policy with a cash value account that grows at a specified fixed rate of interest, guaranteed by the insurance company who issues the policy. Policyholder premiums are not flexible and remain the same during the life of the policy. A whole life policy is the only permanent insurance policy that may offer policyholder's payable dividends as a benefit that can be deposited into the cash value account. Dividends can be used to buy additional insurance coverage, or reduce your premiums. Dividend payments to policyholders are granted yearly but not guaranteed.

Universal Life

Universal Life is known as flexible premium adjustable life insurance and has more flexibility than Whole Life insurance. However, like Whole Life, the cash value account of Universal Life insurance grows at a fixed rate of interest as determined by the insurance company.

Universal life policies offer flexible features in two ways:

1. **Premium payment:** Policyholders are not locked into paying premiums that remains the same during the life of the policy as with whole life insurance. For example, premiums may be skipped or lowered depending on the growth of the cash value account in a Universal Life policy. Also, you may voluntarily increase premiums payments if you desire to save more money in your cash value account for financial freedom. Your policy will offer a maximum savings limit which is the amount of money above and beyond your premiums that you can sock away.

2. **Adjustable death benefit:** The death benefit amount, what your beneficiaries receive, may be decreased, within the policy's limits, as your need for life insurance coverage changes. Your premiums may change and be lowered based on the adjustment.

Variable Universal Life Insurance

Variable Universal Life is similar to Universal Life with one exception. Variable Universal Life insurance offers policyholders the option to invest the cash value account in a wide variety of investment sub accounts tied to the stock market. Subaccount options vary from insurance company to insurance company. Generally all life insurance companies offer policyholders a range of conservative to aggressive investment options. *Variable life insurance is offered by prospectus only. A prospectus is available from your investment professional. The prospectus contains information about the product's features, risks, charges and expenses, and the investment objectives, risks and policies of the underlying portfolios, as well other information about the underlying funding choices. Please read the prospectus and consider this information carefully before investing. Product availability and features may vary by state. All product guarantees are based on the claims-paying ability of the issuing insurance company.*

The amounts allocated to the variable investment options of your account balance are subject to market fluctuations so that, when withdrawn it may be worth more or less than its original value. Past performance is not a guarantee of future results.

Weigh In: What Type of Insurance Should I buy?

Most people struggle with which type of life insurance policy is best for their lifestyle and spending plan. The low costs of group term life insurance coverage at work can tempt you to go the cheap route. In the long run, however, this may not be the best decision for you. The truth is both term and permanent life insurance coverage are worthy of your consideration. Both types of insurance have advantages. A favorable solution may be to have a mix of term and permanent insurance. Having such a combination can lower your overall premiums.

Insurance policies have terms, conditions and exclusions for keeping the policy in place. It is really important to consider having a consultation with an insurance professional to fully assess your needs for life insurance and evaluate your options for coverage. Then place an amount of life insurance in your insurance portfolio that satisfies all or as much of your total need as possible within the confines of your spending plan.

Three Reasons to Consider Term Insurance

1. **A Starter Policy To Protect Your Entire Need:** Because term life insurance is the least expensive type of life insurance plan, it can be a great solution as a "starter policy" that protects your entire need for financial protection.

2. **Temporary Needs:** Term life is a solution suitable to protect temporary financial obligations such as debts or any other future significant expenses.

3. **A Combination with Permanent Life Insurance:** If you're looking for a cost effective way to protect your short term and long term needs for life insurance, having a combination of term and permanent life insurance can be a solution. It may be advisable to consider term life protection to protect your temporary need and provide for your longer term needs using permanent insurance.

Three Reasons to Consider Permanent Insurance

1. **Lifetime Protection:** Permanent life insurance can provide life long protection and is a viable solution for your long term protection needs.

2. **Cash Value Benefit:** Permanent insurance not only pays a death benefit to your beneficiaries, but there is a living benefit for you which is the ability to accumulate cash value on a tax deferred basis. You may take advantage of your cash value account to build financial freedom. *The performance of underlying sub-account funds within the variable life policy are not guaranteed and will fluctuate in value based on market conditions, such that they may lose value. Poor performance of the underlying sub-accounts may necessitate the payment of additional premiums to keep the policy in-force, without which the policy could lapse resulting in potential tax consequences. Withdrawn or borrowed amounts do not participate in the performance of the underlying investment options.*

3. **Flexibility:** Universal and Variable Universal policies offer the option to be flexible when paying premiums and adjusting the death benefit as your needs change.

Weigh In: Isn't What I Have At Work Enough?

There are advantages and disadvantages to having group term life insurance coverage at work.

Advantages of Employer Group Life Insurance:

- Group life insurance premiums are cheap, compared to purchasing an individual policy.

- If you are not insurable based on health conditions, typically you can enroll in a basic amount of group life coverage without any consideration for medical history.
- Group life insurance can be used to supplement your short term need for financial protection.

Disadvantages of Employer Group Life Insurance:
- Your group life at work may not be enough insurance protection for your needs.
- Group life insurance coverage ends when your employment ends.

Group term life insurance is a valuable resource; however, it should be viewed as supplemental life insurance for your short term needs. Just see group life as inexpensive coverage. Don't rely on using group coverage as your primary life insurance. If you wait too long to get life insurance outside of work you run the risk of paying more for insurance premiums as you get older. Young people have an advantage when buying life insurance and that is age and hopefully good health. Permanent and term life insurance premiums are based on your age and health status. The younger and healthier you are, the lower your term and permanent insurance premiums will be. It is advantageous to purchase your primary life insurance coverage outside of work when you are young. This way you can lock in a low rate for premiums that may remain the same during the entire life of the policy.

> **YOUR FINANCIAL FITNESS WORKOUT:**
> **Weigh In Life Insurance**

The cliché says, "We cannot take our money with us when we die." Or can you? Will your loved ones be protected from financial harm when you die or will you take their financial security with you when your life ends? Now that you understand the economic value you bring to the people who depend on you financially, how can you ignore protecting them?

During this workout, I will coach you on how to:

- Assemble the information that you will need for your life insurance needs analysis.
- Take inventory of your current life insurance policies.
- Prepare yourself for a consultation with a life insurance professional.

Follow my lead below and place your information on the worksheet at the end of the financial workout. For this exercise you will need pertinent details about your current life insurance policies and your net worth statement's list of assets and debts. If your life insurance policies are locked away in a safe deposit box or not within reach, you can call the insurance company to get the answers you will need.

Step One: List People Who Depend on You Financially

List the people who depend on you financially and your annual contribution to their lifestyle. For how many years will you need to provide for them financially? Write your answer on the chart on page 174.

People Who Depend On Me Financially	My Annual Contribution	For # of Years
My Family	$	
My Child(ren) {for single or divorced parents}	$	
My Parents	$	
Other person	$	

Protecting your child's college expenses is next. According to the College Board, in 2008, annual college tuition for an in-state public 4 year college averages $6,585 and public out-of-state 4 year college $17,452. These expenses are increasing by 5-6% each year. You may be concerned about planning to protect your child's ability to fund undergraduate and graduate college expenses. If so, include the cost in your needs analysis.

In the next section, list your child's name, the annual cost of tuition and the number of years you are planning to pay for your child's college education. You can research the cost of your preferred college or university on the internet.

My Child's College Fund	Annual Cost	For # of Years
Child #1	$	
Child #2	$	
Child #3	$	

Chapter 6: Weigh In: Protect What You Value   175

Step Two: List Your Liabilities.

Consider any debts that you would like to help your spouse/partner/family pay off and list them on the chart below.

My Liabilities	Total Balance Due
Mortgage	$
Auto	$
Student Loan	$
Credit Cards	$
Other Loans and Debts	$

Step Three: Offset Total Need for Life Insurance Coverage

List your assets that can help your beneficiaries create a reliable income stream or satisfy immediate lump sum money needs at your death. Also list all active life insurance policies that you have in place. This will include employer group term life.

My Assets	Present Value
Savings	$
Bonds	$
Mutual Funds	$
IRA's	$
Retirement Account, 401k, 403b etc.	$
Stocks	$
Real Estate Investments	$
Cash value of life insurance	$

List the name of the insurance company and type of insurance coverage you have. With term also list the # of years left on your term policy.

Name of Insurance Company	Life Insurance That I Have Now	
	Type of Insurance	Amount of Coverage
Ex. My Employer	Group term at work	$ 50,000
Ex. Life Insurance Company	Term	$ 500,000
	Whole Life	$
	Universal Life	$
	Variable Universal Life	$

Step Four: Meet With a Financial Professional

Your next step is to share your information with a financial professional. Ask for a comprehensive consultation to address solutions for your life insurance need. Bring your life insurance worksheet to your meeting. Consider working with a financial professional who represents a reputable financially sound company with an A+ rating or better as reported by www.ambest.com. A.M. Best is a worldwide insurance rating agency with over 100 years of rating and assessing the creditworthiness and financial stability of insurance companies.

Chapter 6: Weigh In: Protect What You Value

People Who Depend On Me Financially	My Annual Contribution	For # of Years
My Family	$	
My Child(ren) {for single or divorced parents}	$	
My Parents	$	
Other person	$	
My Child's College Fund	**Annual Cost**	**For # of Years**
Child #1		
Child #2		
My Liabilities	**Total Balance Due**	
Mortgage	$	
Auto	$	
Student Loan	$	
Credit Cards	$	
My Assets	**Present Value**	
Cash Value of Life Insurance	$	
Savings	$	
Bonds	$	
Mutual Funds	$	
IRA's	$	
Retirement Account, 401k, 403b etc.	$	
Stocks	$	
Life Insurance That I Have Now		
Name of Insurance Company	**Type of Insurance**	**Amount**
Ex. My Employer	Ex. Group term at work	$35,000
Ex. Life Insurance Company	20 Yr Term/15 years left	$250,000
	Whole Life	
	Universal Life	
	Variable Universal Life	
	Term	

Weigh In: Disability Income Insurance

Did you know your most valuable asset is your ability to earn an income?

Here's an example of the total economic value of an income over the course of a person's life . Find your place on the chart below and see how much money is on the table for you. The chart shows:

- The total value of income thru age 65
- With an annual increase of 3% per year
- Including 4% inflation erosion
- Adjusted by Federal tax at 25%

Annual Income					
Your Age Today	$40,000	$60,000	$80,000	$100,000	$120,000
25	$791,585	$1,187,496	$1,583,169	$1,979,080	$2,374,991
30	$753,724	$1,130,699	$1,507,447	$1,884,422	$2,261,397
35	$703,731	$1,055,702	$1,407,462	$1,759,433	$2,111,404
40	$639,448	$959,267	$1,278,895	$1,598,715	$1,918,535

Your income can help you support a lifestyle, achieve your goals, invest, and build wealth. $750,000, $1.1 million, or $1.9 million dollars in earned income over the course of your wage earning years, may be at your disposal. Will you spend it wastefully or are you going to use your money to finance your best life and achieve financial freedom in your lifetime?

Now think. How would you feel if an accident or sickness prevented you from earning money for 1 year, 5 years or for life? How would you replace your total income and keep your household running financially? If you have savings to rely on, your money can easily be spent within six months or so and then what? You'll still have monthly expenses for instance rent, mortgage, food, utilities, car notes and car insurance. If you have children add in expenses for their welfare. You insure your car and your home. Have you thought about insuring your income?

Life's uncertainties have a way of showing up unexpectedly in the form of an untimely illness, an accident, necessary emergency surgery, you name it. A serious illness or injury can harm more than your health; it can have an impact on your financial security. While some people can get by without working for a few months by tapping into their savings, fewer people cannot afford to be out of work on sick leave for an extended period of time. For these reasons, consider including a disability income insurance plan within your insurance portfolio. Disability income insurance replaces a portion of your lost income and helps to close the financial gap when you are unable to work because of a short term or long term disability occurrence.

Disability Income Insurance Basics

Disability insurance is designed to replace a pre-determined percentage of your income, usually 50%-65%, when you are out of work due to an accident or illness. It is a fact; insurance companies will not cover 100% of your income because they want you to have an incentive to return to work. Nonetheless, a percentage of your income to be replaced is better than none; it can serve as a tremendous resource to keep your household running when you do not have a regular pay check coming in.

Do you have disability income insurance? While most people understand the need to have life insurance coverage, the need for disability income insurance is less understood and overlooked. There is a distinct possibility that you may have to deal with a loss of income during a short or long term illness. Those who proactively learn the basics about disability income insurance and plan to protect their income will find themselves in better financial control if or when they need to depend on it. Not having the coverage can have an impact on your personal financial security.

The basics about disability income insurance that you should know are:

- Types of disability income plans
- How to get coverage
- How much coverage do you really need
- Taxation of disability income insurance payments

Types of Disability Income Insurance

There are two types of disability income protection plans each offered separately:

- Short term disability (STD)
- Long term disability (LTD)

Short Term Disability

Short term disability income insurance replaces a percentage of your income by paying a weekly or monthly benefit payment for a benefit period up to 180 days. Once your doctor medically declares you are not able to return to work due to an accident or illness, benefits are payable after meeting a typical 14 day waiting period. The waiting period is a sequence of days beginning with the 1st day you receive your doctor's orders to stay home from work and recuperate. During the waiting period no benefits are paid. At the end of the 180 day benefit period, short term disability payments cease. However if your doctor advises you are still not well enough to return to work at the end of your benefit period, long term disability income insurance coverage kicks in where short term disability protection leaves off. If you do not have LTD, you will be on your own financially.

Long Term Disability

Long term disability income insurance replaces a percentage of income and pays a monthly income benefit payment for a benefit period such as 2 years, 5 years, up to age 65. Like short term disability insurance, LTD has a waiting period, generally 60, 90, 180, or 365 days. The waiting period clock starts counting days beginning with the first day your doctor's orders state do not return to work until medically advisable. As with STD, LTD benefit payments end when the benefit period expires.

How to Get Coverage?

There are two avenues for obtaining disability income insurance:
- Enrolling in a group disability coverage plan
- Purchasing an individual disability income insurance plan

Group Coverage

Group disability insurance policies cover a group of individuals who are affiliated in some way, either through an employer, trade association, or other organization. Employer coverage is the most common avenue pursued mainly because employers already have a disability income insurance plan in place to plug into. An attractive feature of employer provided coverage is that it generally does not require any qualifying questions to enroll; you automatically qualify for coverage.

Many professional associations offer members the opportunity to purchase disability insurance through a group plan. A disability insurance plan offered through professional associations generally base premiums on your age and income. These plans offered by associations are a cost effective option for protecting your income. However, there are draw backs in owning group coverage through associations or employers. With employer plans, if you change professions, the coverage may not follow you. Professional organizations and trade associations reserve the right to cancel offering the coverage to members at any time which is contrary to purchasing an individual plan on your own. Individual plans are guaranteed renewable as long as you pay your premiums.

It is surprising how few numbers of people enrolled in group disability plans at work know how much their benefit would pay out if they were on a short or long term sick leave. Often too, many people do not realize their employer has offered the coverage at work and is paying the premiums for them as an employee benefit.

Chapter 6: Weigh In: Protect What You Value 183

If your employer is offering employer paid disability income coverage or if you voluntarily enrolled in a group disability plan, calculate what your STD and/or LTD benefit payment would be. Have you taken the time to do that yet? You may find your benefit payment may or may not be enough money to cover your household expenses in case you will need to rely on the insurance. Knowing this puts you in a better position to protect your income and address a shortfall ahead of time.

There are 5 ways to address a financial shortfall if temporarily or permanently disabled from working:

1. **Use your savings:** Having 3-6 months of living expenses in savings can help you get by financially if you were out of work for a short period. But, what about a period longer than 6 months? Just know one year out of work may rapidly deplete savings that you built over many years.

2. **Borrow money:** This may create a mountain of debt to remove once you get well and return to work.

3. **Reduce expenses:** If you became disabled, which expenses can be reduced or eliminated from your spending plan?

4. **Social Security:** is available for persons who are disabled and unable to return to work permanently. It isn't easy to qualify for Social Security and doing so may not be resolved timely enough to meet your financial obligations.

4. **Supplement** your group coverage with a individual disability income plan purchased on your own.

Individual Disability Insurance

Individual STD or LTD disability income insurance plans are purchased on your own through qualified insurance professionals. There are reasonable advantages to buying individual disability coverage on your own. For one, you never need to worry about losing coverage if you change jobs. What's more, individual policies may be purchased to piggy back on group coverage that you have at work thereby enriching your income protection.

How Much Coverage Do You Need?

It is recommended to carry disability coverage that will replace at least 50 to 65 percent of your income. Another way to determine how much of a benefit payment you would need is to itemize living expenses that must be paid whether or not you are out on a disability.

Taxation of Disability Income Benefits

Depending on how disability insurance premiums are paid, disability income benefits will either be taxable just like your regular paycheck or paid tax-free. Here's how to ascertain the tax status of your disability benefit:

Your benefit is taxable if:

- Your employer pays the premiums for your group coverage.
- You are paying the premiums via payroll pre-tax deduction.

Your benefit is tax-free if:

- You are paying the premiums for a group or individual plan with after-tax dollars.

The taxation of your benefit is a really important fact to know when computing your benefit because if your benefits are tax-free, you take home more money versus having taxable benefits. If you are unsure whether your group coverage premiums are paid with pre-tax or after tax dollars, refer to your pay stub's itemized deductions columns.

Your Financial Fitness Workout:
Weigh In Disability Insurance

Doesn't it make good sense to insure your income?

Follow my lead below and complete the worksheet at the end of the financial workout as we:

- Review your employer's or professional association group coverage.
- Calculate your benefit.
- Assess monthly expenses vs. monthly disability benefit.
- Assess needs for individual coverage.
- Review your individual policy.

For this financial workout exercise, you will need a copy of the employer's or association's group disability benefit statement that outlines your STD and LTD benefit payment and waiting period . If a current copy is not available for review on your employer's website, contact the human resources department or plan administrator to request a copy be mailed, faxed, or emailed to you. You will also need a copy of your individual disability income policy.

Step One: List Income and Expenses

Disability income insurance protects your ability to keep your household running financially when you are out of work for an extended period because of an accident or illness. So let's first look at your need for protection by examining your income and expenses.

List your annual income and monthly take home pay. Review your spending plan and list your total monthly expenses. Only consider expenses that are absolutely necessary to keep going if you were on sick leave.

Income Protection Needs:	
MY Annual Income	$
MY Monthly Take Home Pay	$
MY Monthly Expenses	$

Next review your employee benefits statement and calculate the Short Term Disability benefit available to you at work. List the waiting period, benefit period, and premium.

Record the pre-tax or after-tax status of your premiums. If your premiums are paid pre-tax, your benefit is taxable. If after-tax it is tax free. Refer to your pay stub for the answer. The answer to the taxation of your disability benefit payment helps you estimate what your "take home benefit payment will be." Consider at least 25% Federal taxes due on benefits paid with pre-tax dollars.

Employer Coverage Short Term Disability	
Monthly Benefit Amount	$
Waiting Period	
Benefit Period	
Premium	$
Pre-tax or After-tax Premium	

Is the monthly STD benefit enough to cover your necessary monthly expenses? Do you have enough savings in place to cover the shortfall during the benefit period? If not, take action now to increase your cash reserve. Consider building 3-6 months of living expenses for those times when you do not have a regular paycheck coming in.

Next review your employee benefits statement and calculate the Long Term Disability benefit available. List the waiting period, benefit period, and pre-tax or after tax premium.

Employer Coverage Long Term Disability	
Monthly Benefit Amount	$
Waiting Period	
Benefit Period	
Premium	$
Pre-tax or After-tax Premium	

Ask yourself if the monthly LTD benefit will be enough to cover monthly expenses? If not, consider meeting with a financial professional to discuss adding an individual LTD plan to your insurance portfolio to protect your income.

Complete the same information for your Individual Disability policy. Stay in tuned with how this coverage may help you during an extended disability occurrence. As your income increases overtime, review your coverage with an insurance professional and decide whether it is best to increase your income protection.

Individual Disability Insurance	STD	LTD
Benefit Amount	$	$
Waiting Period		
Benefit Period		
After tax Insurance Premium	$	$

Your 60 Second Cooling Period

You can rest assured when you are well insured. Young adults you have a valuable advantage to achieve financial freedom in your lifetime and set a precedent for your future generation's benefit. Protecting your living legacy from the possibility of a negative financial setback is paramount so that you may enjoy life with no financial barriers and lead your family and community in a better financial direction.

Income Protection Needs:	
MY Annual Income	$
MY Monthly Take Home Pay	$
MY Monthly Expenses	$
Employer Coverage Short Term Disability	
Monthly Benefit Amount	$
Waiting Period	
Benefit Period	
Premium	$
Pre-tax or After-tax Premium	$
Employer Coverage Long Term Disability	
Monthly Benefit Amount	$
Waiting Period	
Benefit Period	
Premium	$
Pre-tax or After-tax Premium	$

Individual Disability Insurance	STD	LTD
Benefit Amount	$	$
Waiting Period		
Benefit Period		
After tax Insurance Premium	$	$

Chapter 7

What does your legacy say about you?

Your life, my life, everyone's life tells a unique story. We write the story of our life each day. It is our life's story that will go on for years to come. The story of your life at this moment in time is your living legacy. Legacy is often perceived as something that is left behind after a person has passed away. Not so. You don't have to be rich, famous, or wait until you die to have a legacy. Your legacy represents your life's story while you are living, your impact on others whether negative or positive as well as your lasting contribution when your life ends. Beyond your material and financial assets your living legacy may signify your accomplishments, volunteered time, advice, and love. All of it for you to experience and pass it on if that is your desire. Your legacy is also an extension of your philosophies, beliefs and values to your loved ones and community. What does your life story say about you?

I believe everyone desires to live a life of significance and be thought of as a person with good character. Commonly, we want to lovingly impact our family, experience and share a world of interests, inspire others or contribute some kind of way to people within our community. This desire amazingly expands your awareness that you are part of something larger than you wanting to live financially free. The desire to live a life of significance brings into focus you are a part of a meaningful lasting impression. The best way to understand what I am saying is to think of the people closest to you who influenced you and shaped your ideals. People like your grandparents, parents, family members, a mentor, teacher, or someone who took the time to offer you valuable advice. Think of the life stories of ancestors who lived before you. Stories of good cheer, good character, lessons learned and good will that made you proud or inspired you. Think of the lasting impact these people may have made on your life. These meaningful lasting impressions are significant legacies passed on to you. Take a moment to reflect and relive legacies that touched you in a special way.

What would you like for others to remember and appreciate most about you? The beauty of it all is you can decide what your legacy will be and touch lives in a special way too. Envision and decide how you can contribute to the world and be giving of yourself in ways that make you feel good and proud. Then just live the legacy. Every day represent the life story that you want to be told to your children, your family, community, and future generations. This significant outlook on your life not only provides insight on how to change your life for the better, it also presents an opportunity to contribute meaningfully to the lives of people around you. You can bring out the best in the way you live by creating a living legacy that positively reflects you.

> **CHANGE YOUR LIFE FOR THE BETTER FINANCIALLY**
>
> **Simple Step #7:**
> **Create A Living Legacy That Positively Reflects you**

Creating a Living Legacy

There are many instances where people die without passing on family history, accumulated experiences, knowledge, or wealth that may impact generation after generation. If you fail to capture these experiences and gifts in a way that they can be shared, given away or passed on, they lose their value. Worse, it will become insignificant because no one will ever know or benefit from what you have to offer. Unfortunately all too soon things we thought we could never forget, what we dreamed or accomplished, who we are and the places where we are from can be lost in time if not shared or passed on. Creating, preserving, and passing on your legacy can be long-lasting. Your legacy can become a lasting legacy that is emulated and multiplied generation after generation. You may or may not have thought about your life in this significant light. However, this is the power of YOU.

With a little foresight and a little insight, you have the power to inspire people in your world today. Those who come after you can learn from your successes and from your failures. Whether or not you have inherited a financial legacy from your ancestors, you too, have the power to build wealth modestly utilizing wealth building strategies and pass on a financial legacy to your family. There is also power in giving of your time, energy and money socially by contributing to a worthy cause to help others less fortunate than you. Most importantly, you have the power to set an example and share your personal life, faith, encouragement and vision to enable others to build upon a base that you have created during your lifetime. Your lasting impression may give others the inspiration to go and build a life of significance that stretches further than you may have been able.

It also helps to begin creating a living legacy with an acknowledgement of the fact that your life is not meaningless. Every day is your opportunity to make history and influence the future for the better. Often times people focus on individuals who make a huge historic impact forgetting that we too are making history and influencing the future with the way we live our lives. Realize that however your daily life may seem, your life is actually significant and meaningful. How you treat people in each moment, with every interaction, you can have a major impact. In light of this, now is a good time to ask yourself what will your legacy be?

Insights on distinctive ways to create a living legacy that positively reflects your personal, family, financial and socially responsible legacies is the essence of our final financial fitness coaching session together. Understanding the distinction between legacies can help you envision a life of significance uniquely yours that you can create.

Your Personal Legacy

A personal legacy is a gift that you can give which cannot be measured by money. Immeasurable gifts of yourself to others in ways such as enduring relationships, passing on your experiences, family memories, knowledge, and preserving your accomplishments so that you may inform, educate and inspire others are priceless. There are many ways to express and pass on your personal legacy.

For instance:

1. Living according to your values.
2. Displaying random acts of kindness day to day.
3. Demonstrating good character.
4. Offering yourself as a mentor or simply offering good advice.
5. Sharing your successes and how you may have overcome challenges.
6. Setting a positive example of caring for your well being.
7. Being encouraging.
8. Sharing your faith and vision to enable others to carry your torch and build upon a base that you created during your lifetime.

Your Family Legacy

Your family legacy is the story of your family's heritage and history. While many people may have the luxury of hearing stories of ancestors, great grand parents, aunts and uncles, for others these stories may be lost in time. No matter which category you may fall under, beginning with you, consider honoring, documenting and preserving your heritage of family members who are living. Wouldn't it be great for your future generations to be able to enjoy your living family's stories as well as your ancestors' heritage?

Documenting these stories of your family existence and fellowship in real time and researching your family heritage of yesteryear can make a great project that can become a lasting legacy. It can be you who sets an example to honor your family's legacy by passing it on to future generations so that they may know who you are, where they are from and what their family members dreamed or accomplished.

There are unique ways of documenting and preserving your living family's history that can bring joy and inspiration to you, your family and generations to follow. Here are some inspiring ideas that you can consider:

1. Create a dynamic family tree of your living family members. Then make it a fun project to research your genealogy and add your ancestors names and life stories.
2. Keep a journal that documents your pathway in life.
3. Build a library of photo videos from various of stages of your life and the life of your family. Include celebrated moments, weddings, birthdays, anniversaries and other special family events.
4. Craft a scrapbook or memory book designed with photos and other memorabilia. Add stories, captions that can be beautifully bound in a hard or soft cover book.
5. Create an oral history MP3 or audio CD that can be preserved. Oral family history never goes out of style. Imagine the thrill of excitement future generations will enjoy when they hear your voice speak to them.
6. Collectively gather all of the above and build a family legacy

website that can be shared with family members of today and forever on.

Your Financial Legacy

Your financial legacy is a financial gift that you can pass on while you are living or leave behind for your loved ones and future generations to enjoy. One of the most rewarding benefits of modestly accumulating wealth is being able to share it. Your sacrifice, commitment and shared knowledge of wealth building can be passed onto your children, family members and community to help them better prepare for financial freedom. All of this can happen because you have a desire to pass on knowledge and financial resources that will enable them to build, attain and maintain financial security. What's more, your financial values can be emulated and perpetuated.

How well you prepare and build financial freedom ties directly to the kind of financial legacy you can leave. As you increase your knowledge and apply financial fitness to your lifestyle, begin to think about ways you can share the importance of good financial health with your children and community. Envision how your financial legacy may impact your family's financial security. Then simply commit to financial fitness and creating a legacy that reflects you being responsible with your money and building wealth. Ideally, you want to have a holistic strategy to achieve financial freedom which affords you the ability to maintain the lifestyle you deserve in the present while also building a financial legacy that you can gift in the future. A financial professional can help guide you to an appropriate wealth building plan that satisfies your financial legacy goals.

There are three common financial legacy goals pursued by many that may also resonate with you.

1. **The gift of an inheritance:** An inheritance is typically accomplished by naming an heir the beneficiary of your savings, investments, other assets of monetary value and life insurance. Passing on a financial legacy to care for the financial well being of children and loved ones is important to many people. An inheritance can also be an outright gift given while you are living to your loved ones during certain milestone of their life such as a graduation, wedding, or birth of a child.

2. **The gift of an education fund:** The gift of an education fund is invaluable and never goes out of style. Preparing an education fund for a child isn't something to postpone. It's a financial legacy that can be built during a child's early life and passed on by anyone caring for the child's future. College savings plans are typical wealth building vehicles for education funds. Life insurance is also considered to provide for an education fund in the event a parent or guardian dies before the child becomes an adult.

3. **The gift of a charitable donation to an alma mater or favorite non profit organization:** A charitable donation is a profound gesture. Educational institutions and non profits rely on benevolent socially responsible citizens in order to remain in existence. A financial legacy passed on to a favorite cause is a valuable contribution that makes a difference. Commonly financial gifts to favorite causes may be savings, investments, and naming the non profit or alma mater the beneficiary of a life insurance policy.

Your Socially Responsible Legacy

Social responsibility is the act of giving with a sense of responsibility for your family and community. Social responsibility has more to do with serving the well being of others, especially people less fortunate than you, because it is the right thing to do. What if everyone lived life with passion and purpose? And, when your life connects with another you add value to one another's mission. This exemplifies social responsibility in the purest fashion. We all must be held morally accountable for our ability to responsibly take action to positively impact the life of another person.

Being socially responsible and serving others creates a change reaction. Through service, we have the "ability" to "respond" to the needs of someone else. As we do, we can change a life and in doing so we change ourselves for the better because we did the right thing. We are in this world to make it a better place for you, me and for others. We are on this planet to be adventurous with our life and explore our life's passion and purpose. We cannot fulfill our passion and purpose alone. We need each other. We need to commit to our living legacy and contribute to the legacy of others, which also means incorporating "service" into our lifestyle.

Community service projects, giving campaigns, and volunteerism are the most common ways to engage in social service and create a social responsibility legacy. Unique projects, campaigns and volunteering opportunities may fall under one of the following categories:

- Community Service Projects
- Giving Goods and Donating Services

- Going on A Mission Trip
- Doing Good Deeds For Others

Deciding when, where, and how you can incorporate service into your lifestyle can be a fun and exciting experience. People serve others and their community for a wide variety of reasons totally based on their respective personality, skills, level of compassion for a cause, and personal satisfaction in knowing that their service will make a difference. There are many service outlets where you can begin to create a social responsibility legacy. Options can be working with non profits, churches, and volunteer service oriented agencies within your local community. Additionally, if you are feeling adventurous you can use the internet to search social service opportunities that support special causes and national or global initiatives. Make it a fun and exciting experience for you no matter how you decide to serve. When deciding on social service organizations consider basing your decision on the personal satisfaction that you will receive. It is then you will know you made a great choice for your efforts.

Because social responsibility creates a change reaction amongst all parties involved, it is ok to want some additional benefits for yourself from being socially responsible. There is a long tradition of seeing service and volunteering as a form of charity based on altruism. However, the best act of social responsibility involves the desire to serve others while fulfilling motivations that may benefit you as well. For instance, the motivation that you may have in selecting when, where and why you would like to serve may not only be to help others. You may have some special reason of your own that may benefit you such as:

- To get to know a community
- To build your resume
- To gain leadership skills
- For recognition
- To travel
- To learn something new
- To make new friends
- To keep your skills alive
- To be an agent of change
- To demonstrate commitment to a cause based on a personal experience
- To stand up and be counted
- To feel needed, challenged, or proud

As long as you are sincerely serving, it is perfectly ok to experience an exchange that creates a change reaction in you too. In fact, if you feel the rewards of serving others your commitment to a social cause or project may strengthen. You will continue to serve as long as your efforts are accomplishing something, your talents are appreciated, and you can see the benefits to both the recipient of your service and to yourself.

You may have already experienced what it is like to feel good about helping to feed the homeless, donate warm clothing in the winter to families in need, travel with your church to help an unfortunate community or some other type of service involvement. When it is all said and done, it really does feel good to be socially responsible and know that you can contribute to changing another person's life for the better. Feel good when doing good is my mantra. Create your own mantra and wonderful impactful experiences when doing good for others. Make a lasting legacy impression.

> **YOUR FINANCIAL FITNESS WORKOUT:**
> **Create a Living Legacy that Positively Reflects you**

There is beauty and wonderment in having the vision of your living legacy; however, your vision can only come to life when you live with the individual responsibility to make it a reality and stamp it as an enduring contribution. Your life is shaped in moments of contribution. Every day you have a new opportunity to create and shape your own story in the world. What is the story that you want to be told about you? Will your story be documented by photos, videos, or a family blog? Will you be remembered as a mentor who offered valuable advice, provider of family financial security in the present and for future generations, or known for your philanthropic endeavors and a life of service in your community? The choice is up to you. The beauty of it all is you can decide what your living legacy will be.

Here's your starting point:
- Acknowledge your desire to touch people's lives in a special way.
- Commit to making this world a better place as others have prepared the world for you.

- Envision what your legacy will look like.
- Create it.
- Live it.

The Workout: Review the distinction between legacies offered in this chapter. And begin to envision how you can build upon the base that I've given you to get started. Consider ways to enjoy sharing and preserving the story of your life with your living family members for future generations to enjoy. It can be you who sets an example to honor your legacy by preserving and passing it on so that your future generations may know who you are, where they are from and what their family members dreamed or accomplished.

1. On a sheet of paper write "My Legacy."
2. Write the vision of your multi-faceted legacy.
   - Personal
   - Family
   - Financial
   - Socially responsible
3. Create a planned approach to build your envisioned legacies in such a way that your involvement will cause a change reaction. And most of all choose an enjoyable creative way to preserve your legacy and make it lasting.
4. Have fun enjoying your multi-faceted legacy plans, your life and living it. Over time, increase your commitment to build upon your contributions to the lives of others. One positive step at a time, one contribution at a time, taking responsibility each time can create a living legacy that you can be proud of.

Your 60 Second Cooling Period

We've actually come full circle in our financial coaching sessions in that we've discussed living life at your best by building a living legacy that positively reflects you. Lifestyle comes first. Always remember that. I am grateful for the opportunity to speak with you through the pages of this book. My hope is that I made a lasting impression. My mission was to inspire you to live a life of significance without sacrificing your financial well being. Was I successful in creating a change reaction through this exchange with you? I hope so. Take good care of your financial health and value financial security. You have the power to change your life for the better financially. Its not can this book change your life, but can you? Be abundantly blessed. Yoli.

Notes

Notes

Notes

Notes

Made in the USA
Lexington, KY
19 December 2011